50 Australian Cake Recipes for Home

By: Kelly Johnson

Table of Contents

- Lamingtons
- Pavlova
- Anzac biscuits
- Tim Tam cake
- Wattleseed cake
- Macadamia nut cake
- Lemon myrtle cake
- Kakadu plum cake
- Finger lime cake
- Passionfruit sponge cake
- Eucalyptus honey cake
- Bush tomato cake
- Tasmanian apple cake
- Pumpkin and ginger cake
- Salted caramel mud cake
- Raspberry and white chocolate mud cake
- Lemon cheesecake
- Chocolate ripple cake
- Bush tucker fruitcake
- Meringue roulade
- Peach Melba cake
- Cherry ripe cheesecake
- Beetroot and chocolate cake
- Date and walnut cake
- Lamington cake
- Lemon curd cake
- Mint slice cake
- Black forest cake
- Blueberry and almond cake
- Mango and coconut cake
- Pineapple upside-down cake
- Vanilla slice
- Passionfruit tart
- Caramel slice
- Coffee cake

- Neenish tart
- Scones
- Fairy bread
- Honeycomb cake
- Raspberry friand
- White chocolate and macadamia cake
- Marmalade cake
- Strawberry sponge cake
- Peanut butter cake
- Banana cake
- Pistachio and rosewater cake
- Carrot cake
- Fig and almond cake
- Gingerbread
- Rum ball cake

Lamingtons

Ingredients:

For the sponge cake:

- 1 cup (200g) caster sugar
- 1 teaspoon vanilla extract
- 4 large eggs
- 2 cups (250g) self-raising flour
- 1/4 teaspoon salt
- 1/2 cup (125ml) milk
- 125g unsalted butter, melted and cooled

For the chocolate icing:

- 3 cups (360g) icing sugar (powdered sugar)
- 1/3 cup (30g) cocoa powder
- 1 tablespoon unsalted butter, melted
- 1/2 cup (125ml) milk
- 3 cups (240g) desiccated coconut, for coating

Instructions:

1. **Preheat oven and prepare baking tin:**
   - Preheat your oven to 180°C (350°F). Grease and line a 20cm x 30cm (8in x 12in) rectangular baking tin with parchment paper.
2. **Prepare the sponge cake:**
   - In a large bowl, beat the caster sugar, vanilla extract, and eggs together until pale and creamy.
   - Sift the self-raising flour and salt together. Gradually add the flour mixture to the egg mixture, alternating with the milk, beginning and ending with the flour mixture. Mix until just combined.
   - Gently fold in the melted butter until smooth and well combined.
3. **Bake the sponge cake:**
   - Pour the batter into the prepared baking tin and spread it out evenly.
   - Bake in the preheated oven for 25-30 minutes or until a skewer inserted into the center of the cake comes out clean.
   - Remove from the oven and allow the cake to cool completely in the tin.
4. **Cut and prepare for coating:**
   - Once cooled, gently remove the cake from the tin and transfer it to a cutting board. Cut the cake into squares or rectangles of your desired size (traditionally about 5cm x 5cm or 2in x 2in).
5. **Make the chocolate icing:**

- Sift the icing sugar and cocoa powder into a large bowl. Add the melted butter and milk, and stir until smooth and well combined. The icing should be thick but pourable.

6. **Coat the Lamingtons:**
   - Place the desiccated coconut in a shallow bowl.
   - Using two forks or skewers, dip each piece of sponge cake into the chocolate icing, ensuring it is evenly coated.
   - Allow any excess icing to drip off briefly, then roll the coated cake in the desiccated coconut until completely covered.

7. **Set and serve:**
   - Place the coated Lamingtons on a wire rack to set for at least 30 minutes, or until the icing has hardened.
   - Serve and enjoy! Lamingtons are best enjoyed fresh on the day they are made, but they can be stored in an airtight container at room temperature for up to 3 days.

Enjoy your homemade Lamingtons! They're a delightful treat with a perfect balance of chocolate, coconut, and fluffy sponge cake.

Pavlova

Ingredients:

- 4 large egg whites, at room temperature
- 1 cup (200g) caster sugar
- 1 teaspoon white vinegar or lemon juice
- 1 teaspoon cornflour (cornstarch)
- 1/2 teaspoon vanilla extract
- 300ml thickened cream, whipped (for topping)
- Fresh fruits (such as strawberries, kiwi, passionfruit, or berries) for topping

Instructions:

1. **Preheat oven and prepare baking tray:**
   - Preheat your oven to 150°C (300°F). Line a baking tray with baking paper.
2. **Prepare the meringue:**
   - In a clean, dry bowl, use an electric mixer to beat the egg whites on medium-high speed until soft peaks form.
   - Gradually add the caster sugar, a tablespoon at a time, beating well after each addition. Continue beating until the sugar has dissolved and the mixture is thick and glossy. You can test this by rubbing a bit of the mixture between your fingers – it should feel smooth, not gritty.
   - Add the vinegar or lemon juice, cornflour, and vanilla extract. Beat briefly until just combined.
3. **Shape and bake the Pavlova:**
   - Spoon the meringue mixture onto the prepared baking tray, shaping it into a circle or oval with a slight indentation in the center to hold the toppings.
   - Smooth the sides and top gently with a spatula.
4. **Bake the Pavlova:**
   - Place the Pavlova in the preheated oven and immediately reduce the temperature to 120°C (250°F).
   - Bake for 1 hour to 1 hour 15 minutes, or until the Pavlova is dry to the touch and a pale cream color. It should sound hollow when tapped on the base.
5. **Cool the Pavlova:**
   - Turn off the oven and leave the Pavlova to cool completely in the oven with the door slightly ajar.
6. **Assemble the Pavlova:**
   - Once cooled, carefully transfer the Pavlova to a serving platter or cake stand.
   - Whip the cream until thick and spread it over the top of the Pavlova.
   - Arrange fresh fruits over the whipped cream. Popular choices include strawberries, kiwi fruit, passionfruit pulp, raspberries, blueberries, or any seasonal fruits you prefer.
7. **Serve and enjoy:**

- Serve the Pavlova immediately after assembling to enjoy the crisp exterior and soft, marshmallow-like interior.

Pavlova is best enjoyed fresh, as the meringue base can soften over time due to the moisture from the whipped cream and fruits. It's a delightful dessert that's light, airy, and perfect for special occasions or gatherings.

Anzac biscuits

Ingredients:

- 1 cup (150g) plain flour
- 1 cup (90g) rolled oats
- 3/4 cup (150g) brown sugar
- 1/2 cup (40g) desiccated coconut
- 125g unsalted butter
- 2 tablespoons golden syrup (or substitute with honey)
- 1/2 teaspoon bicarbonate of soda (baking soda)
- 1 tablespoon boiling water

Instructions:

1. **Preheat oven:**
   - Preheat your oven to 160°C (320°F) fan-forced. Line baking trays with baking paper.
2. **Combine dry ingredients:**
   - In a large bowl, mix together the plain flour, rolled oats, brown sugar, and desiccated coconut.
3. **Melt butter and syrup:**
   - In a small saucepan, melt the butter and golden syrup (or honey) over low heat until combined.
4. **Dissolve baking soda:**
   - In a small bowl, combine the bicarbonate of soda with the boiling water, then add this mixture to the melted butter and syrup mixture. It will froth up.
5. **Combine wet and dry ingredients:**
   - Pour the melted butter mixture into the dry ingredients and stir until well combined and the mixture forms a sticky dough.
6. **Shape and bake:**
   - Roll tablespoonfuls of the mixture into balls and place them on the lined baking trays, leaving space between each biscuit to allow for spreading.
7. **Bake:**
   - Flatten each ball slightly with your fingers or a fork.
   - Bake in the preheated oven for 12-15 minutes or until golden brown. The biscuits will still be soft when they come out of the oven but will firm up as they cool.
8. **Cool and store:**
   - Allow the Anzac biscuits to cool on the trays for 5 minutes before transferring them to a wire rack to cool completely.
   - Once cooled, store the Anzac biscuits in an airtight container at room temperature. They should keep well for up to 1-2 weeks (if they last that long!).

Enjoy these delicious Anzac biscuits with a cup of tea or coffee, and appreciate their historical significance as you indulge in this Australian classic!

Tim Tam cake

Ingredients:

For the cake:

- 200g unsalted butter, softened
- 1 cup (200g) caster sugar
- 3 large eggs
- 1 teaspoon vanilla extract
- 1 and 3/4 cups (220g) self-raising flour
- 1/4 cup (30g) cocoa powder
- 1/2 cup (125ml) milk

For the Tim Tam filling:

- 200g Tim Tam biscuits, crushed (plus extra for decorating)
- 1 cup (250ml) thickened cream
- 200g dark chocolate, chopped

For the chocolate ganache:

- 200g dark chocolate, chopped
- 1 cup (250ml) thickened cream

Instructions:

1. **Make the cake:**
    - Preheat your oven to 180°C (350°F). Grease and line two 20cm (8-inch) round cake pans with parchment paper.
    - In a large mixing bowl, cream together the softened butter and caster sugar until light and fluffy.
    - Add the eggs, one at a time, beating well after each addition. Add the vanilla extract and mix until combined.
    - Sift the self-raising flour and cocoa powder together. Fold half of the flour mixture into the creamed mixture, then fold in the milk. Finally, fold in the remaining flour mixture until just combined.
    - Divide the batter evenly between the prepared cake pans and smooth the tops with a spatula.
    - Bake in the preheated oven for 25-30 minutes or until a skewer inserted into the center comes out clean.
    - Remove the cakes from the oven and allow them to cool in the pans for 10 minutes before transferring them to a wire rack to cool completely.
2. **Prepare the Tim Tam filling:**
    - Place the crushed Tim Tam biscuits in a bowl.

- In a small saucepan, heat the thickened cream until it just begins to simmer. Remove from heat and pour over the chopped dark chocolate in a heatproof bowl. Let it sit for 1-2 minutes, then stir until smooth and well combined.
- Pour the chocolate mixture over the crushed Tim Tams and stir until the biscuits are completely coated. Set aside to cool and thicken slightly.

3. **Assemble the cake:**
   - Place one cooled cake layer on a serving plate or cake stand.
   - Spread the Tim Tam filling evenly over the top of the cake layer.
   - Place the second cake layer on top and gently press down.

4. **Make the chocolate ganache:**
   - In a small saucepan, heat the thickened cream until it just begins to simmer.
   - Remove from heat and pour over the chopped dark chocolate in a heatproof bowl. Let it sit for 1-2 minutes, then stir until smooth and glossy.

5. **Decorate the cake:**
   - Pour the chocolate ganache over the top of the assembled cake, allowing it to drip down the sides.
   - Decorate with additional crushed Tim Tam biscuits on top, if desired.

6. **Chill and serve:**
   - Place the cake in the refrigerator for at least 30 minutes to allow the ganache to set.
   - Slice and serve chilled. Enjoy the rich and indulgent Tim Tam cake!

This Tim Tam cake is sure to be a hit with chocolate lovers and fans of these iconic Australian biscuits. It combines moist chocolate cake layers with a creamy Tim Tam filling and decadent chocolate ganache for a truly irresistible dessert experience.

Wattleseed cake

Ingredients:

For the cake:

- 1 cup (250ml) milk
- 2 tablespoons ground roasted wattleseed
- 200g unsalted butter, softened
- 1 cup (200g) caster sugar
- 3 large eggs
- 1 teaspoon vanilla extract
- 2 cups (250g) self-raising flour
- 1/2 cup (60g) almond meal (ground almonds)
- Pinch of salt

For the wattleseed syrup:

- 1/2 cup (125ml) water
- 1/2 cup (100g) caster sugar
- 1 tablespoon ground roasted wattleseed

For garnish (optional):

- Whipped cream or mascarpone
- Fresh berries or fruit slices

Instructions:

1. **Prepare the wattleseed milk:**
    - In a small saucepan, heat the milk until just simmering. Remove from heat and stir in the ground roasted wattleseed. Let it steep for 10-15 minutes, then strain through a fine sieve. Set aside to cool.
2. **Make the cake:**
    - Preheat your oven to 180°C (350°F). Grease and line a 20cm (8-inch) round cake tin with parchment paper.
    - In a large mixing bowl, cream together the softened butter and caster sugar until light and fluffy.
    - Add the eggs, one at a time, beating well after each addition. Add the vanilla extract and mix until combined.
    - Fold in the self-raising flour, almond meal, and salt until just combined.
    - Gradually add the cooled wattleseed-infused milk, mixing until smooth and well combined.
3. **Bake the cake:**
    - Pour the batter into the prepared cake tin and smooth the top with a spatula.

- Bake in the preheated oven for 45-50 minutes, or until a skewer inserted into the center of the cake comes out clean.
- Remove from the oven and let the cake cool in the tin for 10 minutes before transferring it to a wire rack to cool completely.

4. **Make the wattleseed syrup:**
   - In a small saucepan, combine the water, caster sugar, and ground roasted wattleseed. Bring to a boil, stirring until the sugar has dissolved.
   - Reduce the heat and simmer for 5 minutes, then remove from heat and let it cool slightly.

5. **Assemble and serve:**
   - Once the cake has cooled completely, place it on a serving plate or cake stand.
   - Pierce the top of the cake all over with a skewer or fork.
   - Spoon the warm wattleseed syrup evenly over the cake, allowing it to soak in. Reserve a little syrup for serving.
   - Optionally, garnish the cake with whipped cream or mascarpone and fresh berries or fruit slices.

6. **Serve and enjoy:**
   - Slice the wattleseed cake and serve with a drizzle of reserved wattleseed syrup.

This wattleseed cake is wonderfully fragrant and has a unique flavor profile that celebrates native Australian ingredients. It's perfect for special occasions or as a delightful treat any time you want to enjoy something truly Australian.

Macadamia nut cake

Ingredients:

For the cake:

- 1 cup (225g) unsalted butter, softened
- 1 cup (200g) granulated sugar
- 1 cup (200g) brown sugar, packed
- 4 large eggs
- 1 teaspoon vanilla extract
- 2 cups (250g) all-purpose flour
- 2 teaspoons baking powder
- 1/2 teaspoon baking soda
- 1/2 teaspoon salt
- 1 cup (250ml) buttermilk (or 1 cup milk mixed with 1 tablespoon vinegar or lemon juice)
- 1 cup (125g) macadamia nuts, chopped

For the macadamia nut frosting:

- 1/2 cup (115g) unsalted butter, softened
- 3 cups (360g) powdered sugar (icing sugar)
- 1 teaspoon vanilla extract
- 2-3 tablespoons milk or cream
- 1/2 cup (60g) macadamia nuts, chopped (for decoration)

Instructions:

1. **Preheat oven and prepare baking pans:**
    - Preheat your oven to 350°F (175°C). Grease and flour two 9-inch (23cm) round cake pans, or line them with parchment paper.
2. **Prepare the cake batter:**
    - In a large mixing bowl, cream together the softened butter, granulated sugar, and brown sugar until light and fluffy.
    - Add the eggs, one at a time, beating well after each addition. Stir in the vanilla extract.
    - In a separate bowl, sift together the flour, baking powder, baking soda, and salt.
    - Gradually add the dry ingredients to the creamed mixture, alternating with the buttermilk, beginning and ending with the flour mixture. Mix until just combined.
    - Fold in the chopped macadamia nuts until evenly distributed throughout the batter.
3. **Bake the cake:**
    - Divide the batter evenly between the prepared cake pans and smooth the tops with a spatula.

- Bake in the preheated oven for 25-30 minutes, or until a toothpick inserted into the center of the cakes comes out clean.
- Remove from the oven and let the cakes cool in the pans for 10 minutes before transferring them to wire racks to cool completely.

4. **Make the macadamia nut frosting:**
    - In a mixing bowl, beat the softened butter until creamy.
    - Gradually add the powdered sugar, one cup at a time, beating well after each addition.
    - Stir in the vanilla extract.
    - Add milk or cream, one tablespoon at a time, until the frosting reaches your desired consistency for spreading.

5. **Assemble the cake:**
    - Place one cake layer on a serving plate or cake stand. Spread a layer of frosting over the top.
    - Place the second cake layer on top and spread the remaining frosting over the top and sides of the cake.
    - Sprinkle the chopped macadamia nuts over the top of the cake for decoration.

6. **Chill and serve:**
    - Chill the cake in the refrigerator for about 30 minutes to allow the frosting to set.
    - Slice and serve the delicious macadamia nut cake! Enjoy its rich, nutty flavor and moist texture.

This macadamia nut cake is perfect for any occasion, from birthdays to gatherings with friends and family. It celebrates the wonderful flavor of macadamia nuts and is sure to impress anyone who tries it!

Lemon myrtle cake

Ingredients:

For the cake:

- 1 cup (225g) unsalted butter, softened
- 1 and 1/2 cups (300g) granulated sugar
- 4 large eggs
- 2 cups (250g) self-raising flour
- 1/2 cup (60g) almond meal (ground almonds)
- 1/2 cup (125ml) milk
- Zest of 2 lemons
- 1 tablespoon lemon myrtle powder (or finely ground lemon myrtle leaves)
- 1 teaspoon vanilla extract

For the lemon myrtle syrup:

- Juice of 2 lemons
- 1/2 cup (100g) granulated sugar
- 1 tablespoon lemon myrtle powder (or finely ground lemon myrtle leaves)
- 1/2 cup (125ml) water

For the lemon myrtle glaze (optional):

- 1 cup (120g) icing sugar (powdered sugar)
- 1-2 tablespoons lemon juice
- Lemon myrtle powder for dusting (optional)

Instructions:

1. **Preheat oven and prepare baking pan:**
   - Preheat your oven to 350°F (175°C). Grease and line a 9-inch (23cm) round cake pan with parchment paper.
2. **Make the cake batter:**
   - In a large mixing bowl, cream together the softened butter and granulated sugar until light and fluffy.
   - Add the eggs, one at a time, beating well after each addition.
   - Stir in the vanilla extract, lemon zest, and lemon myrtle powder (or ground leaves).
   - Gradually add the self-raising flour and almond meal, alternating with the milk, beginning and ending with the flour mixture. Mix until just combined.
3. **Bake the cake:**
   - Pour the batter into the prepared cake pan and smooth the top with a spatula.

- Bake in the preheated oven for 45-50 minutes, or until a toothpick inserted into the center of the cake comes out clean.
- Remove from the oven and let the cake cool in the pan for 10 minutes before transferring it to a wire rack to cool completely.

4. **Make the lemon myrtle syrup:**
   - In a small saucepan, combine the lemon juice, granulated sugar, lemon myrtle powder (or leaves), and water.
   - Bring to a boil over medium heat, stirring occasionally, until the sugar has dissolved.
   - Reduce the heat and simmer for 5 minutes, then remove from heat and let it cool slightly.

5. **Apply the lemon myrtle syrup:**
   - While the cake is still warm, use a skewer or fork to poke holes all over the top of the cake.
   - Slowly drizzle the warm lemon myrtle syrup over the cake, allowing it to soak in. Reserve a little syrup for brushing on later if desired.

6. **Make the lemon myrtle glaze (optional):**
   - In a small bowl, whisk together the icing sugar and lemon juice until smooth and glossy. Adjust consistency by adding more lemon juice if needed.

7. **Glaze the cake (optional):**
   - Once the cake has cooled completely and the syrup has soaked in, drizzle the lemon myrtle glaze over the top of the cake.

8. **Serve and enjoy:**
   - Optionally, dust the top of the cake with a light sprinkling of lemon myrtle powder for extra flavor and decoration.
   - Slice and serve the lemon myrtle cake. Enjoy its aromatic citrusy flavor and moist texture!

This lemon myrtle cake is a wonderful way to showcase the unique flavors of Australia's native lemon myrtle plant. It's perfect for afternoon tea, special occasions, or anytime you want to enjoy a delightful and fragrant dessert.

Kakadu plum cake

Ingredients:

For the cake:

- 1 cup (225g) unsalted butter, softened
- 1 cup (200g) granulated sugar
- 4 large eggs
- 2 cups (250g) self-raising flour
- 1/2 cup (60g) almond meal (ground almonds)
- 1/2 cup (125ml) milk
- Zest of 1 lemon
- 1/2 cup Kakadu plum puree (about 6-8 Kakadu plums, seeds removed and blended)
- 1 teaspoon vanilla extract

For the Kakadu plum glaze:

- 1/2 cup Kakadu plum puree
- 1/2 cup (100g) granulated sugar
- Juice of 1 lemon

For garnish (optional):

- Kakadu plum slices or wedges
- Lemon zest or Kakadu plum powder

Instructions:

1. **Prepare Kakadu plum puree:**
   - To make Kakadu plum puree, blend Kakadu plums (seeds removed) in a blender or food processor until smooth. You may need to add a little water to help with blending.
2. **Preheat oven and prepare baking pan:**
   - Preheat your oven to 350°F (175°C). Grease and line a 9-inch (23cm) round cake pan with parchment paper.
3. **Make the cake batter:**
   - In a large mixing bowl, cream together the softened butter and granulated sugar until light and fluffy.
   - Add the eggs, one at a time, beating well after each addition.
   - Stir in the vanilla extract, lemon zest, and Kakadu plum puree.
   - Gradually add the self-raising flour and almond meal, alternating with the milk, beginning and ending with the flour mixture. Mix until just combined.
4. **Bake the cake:**
   - Pour the batter into the prepared cake pan and smooth the top with a spatula.

- Bake in the preheated oven for 45-50 minutes, or until a toothpick inserted into the center of the cake comes out clean.
- Remove from the oven and let the cake cool in the pan for 10 minutes before transferring it to a wire rack to cool completely.

5. **Make the Kakadu plum glaze:**
   - In a small saucepan, combine the Kakadu plum puree, granulated sugar, and lemon juice.
   - Bring to a boil over medium heat, stirring constantly until the sugar has dissolved.
   - Reduce the heat and simmer for 5-7 minutes, stirring occasionally, until the glaze thickens slightly.
6. **Apply the Kakadu plum glaze:**
   - While the cake is still warm, brush the Kakadu plum glaze evenly over the top of the cake.
7. **Garnish (optional):**
   - Garnish the cake with Kakadu plum slices or wedges, and sprinkle with lemon zest or Kakadu plum powder for extra flavor and decoration.
8. **Serve and enjoy:**
   - Slice and serve the Kakadu plum cake. Enjoy its unique tart flavor and the fruity goodness of Kakadu plums!

This Kakadu plum cake is a wonderful way to celebrate Australian native ingredients and is sure to be a delightful treat for any occasion.

Finger lime cake

Ingredients:

For the cake:

- 1 cup (225g) unsalted butter, softened
- 1 cup (200g) granulated sugar
- 4 large eggs
- 2 cups (250g) self-raising flour
- 1/2 cup (60g) almond meal (ground almonds)
- 1/2 cup (125ml) milk
- Zest of 2 limes
- Juice of 1 lime
- 2-3 finger limes, pulp removed and seeds discarded
- 1 teaspoon vanilla extract

For the finger lime glaze:

- Pulp of 2-3 finger limes (about 1-2 tablespoons)
- 1 cup (120g) icing sugar (powdered sugar)
- Juice of 1 lime

For garnish (optional):

- Slices or wedges of finger limes
- Lime zest

Instructions:

1. **Prepare the finger lime pulp:**
   - Cut the finger limes in half and scoop out the pulp using a spoon. Discard the seeds. Set aside the pulp for the cake and the glaze.
2. **Preheat oven and prepare baking pan:**
   - Preheat your oven to 350°F (175°C). Grease and line a 9-inch (23cm) round cake pan with parchment paper.
3. **Make the cake batter:**
   - In a large mixing bowl, cream together the softened butter and granulated sugar until light and fluffy.
   - Add the eggs, one at a time, beating well after each addition.
   - Stir in the vanilla extract, lime zest, lime juice, and finger lime pulp.
   - Gradually add the self-raising flour and almond meal, alternating with the milk, beginning and ending with the flour mixture. Mix until just combined.
4. **Bake the cake:**
   - Pour the batter into the prepared cake pan and smooth the top with a spatula.

- Bake in the preheated oven for 45-50 minutes, or until a toothpick inserted into the center of the cake comes out clean.
- Remove from the oven and let the cake cool in the pan for 10 minutes before transferring it to a wire rack to cool completely.

5. **Make the finger lime glaze:**
    - In a small bowl, combine the finger lime pulp, icing sugar, and lime juice. Mix until smooth and well combined.

6. **Apply the finger lime glaze:**
    - While the cake is still warm, poke holes all over the top of the cake using a skewer or fork.
    - Drizzle the finger lime glaze evenly over the top of the cake, allowing it to soak in and drip down the sides.

7. **Garnish (optional):**
    - Garnish the cake with slices or wedges of finger limes and lime zest for extra flavor and decoration.

8. **Serve and enjoy:**
    - Slice and serve the finger lime cake. Enjoy its refreshing citrus flavor and the delightful bursts of finger lime caviar!

This finger lime cake is a wonderful dessert that celebrates the unique flavors of Australian finger limes. It's perfect for any occasion and is sure to impress with its vibrant citrusy taste and beautiful presentation.

Passionfruit sponge cake

Ingredients:

For the sponge cake:

- 4 large eggs, at room temperature
- 3/4 cup (150g) caster sugar
- 1 teaspoon vanilla extract
- 1 cup (125g) self-raising flour
- Pinch of salt
- 2 tablespoons passionfruit pulp (about 2-3 passionfruits)
- Zest of 1 lemon

For the passionfruit filling:

- 1/2 cup (120ml) thickened cream
- 1/4 cup (60g) icing sugar (powdered sugar)
- 1/2 cup passionfruit pulp (about 4-5 passionfruits)

For garnish (optional):

- Fresh passionfruit seeds
- Icing sugar (powdered sugar), for dusting

Instructions:

1. **Preheat oven and prepare baking pan:**
    - Preheat your oven to 180°C (350°F). Grease and line two 8-inch (20cm) round cake pans with parchment paper.
2. **Make the sponge cake:**
    - In a large mixing bowl, beat the eggs and caster sugar together with an electric mixer until pale, thick, and doubled in volume. This will take about 5-7 minutes.
    - Beat in the vanilla extract.
    - Sift the self-raising flour and salt over the egg mixture. Gently fold in using a spatula until just combined. Be careful not to overmix to maintain the lightness of the sponge.
    - Fold in the passionfruit pulp and lemon zest gently until evenly distributed.
    - Divide the batter evenly between the prepared cake pans and smooth the tops with a spatula.
3. **Bake the sponge cakes:**
    - Bake in the preheated oven for 15-20 minutes, or until the cakes are golden brown and spring back when lightly touched in the center.
    - Remove from the oven and let the cakes cool in the pans for 5 minutes before transferring them to wire racks to cool completely.

4. **Make the passionfruit filling:**
    - In a mixing bowl, whip the thickened cream and icing sugar together until stiff peaks form.
    - Gently fold in the passionfruit pulp until well combined.
5. **Assemble the cake:**
    - Place one sponge cake layer on a serving plate or cake stand.
    - Spread the passionfruit cream filling evenly over the top of the cake layer.
    - Place the second sponge cake layer on top and gently press down.
6. **Garnish (optional):**
    - Scatter fresh passionfruit seeds over the top of the cake for decoration.
    - Dust with a light sprinkling of icing sugar (powdered sugar) for an extra touch of sweetness.
7. **Serve and enjoy:**
    - Slice and serve the passionfruit sponge cake. Enjoy the light and fluffy texture with the tangy sweetness of passionfruit!

This passionfruit sponge cake is perfect for afternoon tea, parties, or any occasion where you want to impress with a delightful tropical-flavored dessert. It's refreshing, light, and bursting with tropical flavor from the passionfruit pulp.

Eucalyptus honey cake

Ingredients:

For the cake:

- 1 cup (225g) unsalted butter, softened
- 1 cup (200g) granulated sugar
- 4 large eggs
- 1 teaspoon vanilla extract
- 2 cups (250g) all-purpose flour
- 2 teaspoons baking powder
- 1/2 teaspoon baking soda
- 1/4 teaspoon salt
- 1/2 cup (125ml) buttermilk (or 1/2 cup milk mixed with 1 tablespoon vinegar or lemon juice)
- 1/2 cup eucalyptus honey
- Zest of 1 lemon (optional)

For the honey glaze:

- 1/4 cup (60ml) eucalyptus honey
- 1-2 tablespoons hot water

For garnish (optional):

- Sliced almonds or chopped nuts
- Fresh eucalyptus leaves (cleaned and dried)

Instructions:

1. **Preheat oven and prepare baking pan:**
    - Preheat your oven to 350°F (175°C). Grease and flour a 9-inch (23cm) round cake pan or line it with parchment paper.
2. **Make the cake batter:**
    - In a large mixing bowl, cream together the softened butter and granulated sugar until light and fluffy.
    - Add the eggs, one at a time, beating well after each addition. Stir in the vanilla extract and lemon zest (if using).
    - In a separate bowl, sift together the all-purpose flour, baking powder, baking soda, and salt.
    - Gradually add the dry ingredients to the creamed mixture, alternating with the buttermilk, beginning and ending with the flour mixture. Mix until just combined.
    - Stir in the eucalyptus honey until evenly distributed throughout the batter.
3. **Bake the cake:**

- Pour the batter into the prepared cake pan and smooth the top with a spatula.
- Bake in the preheated oven for 30-35 minutes, or until a toothpick inserted into the center of the cake comes out clean.
- Remove from the oven and let the cake cool in the pan for 10 minutes before transferring it to a wire rack to cool completely.

4. **Make the honey glaze:**
    - In a small bowl, combine the eucalyptus honey and hot water. Stir until smooth.
5. **Apply the honey glaze:**
    - While the cake is still warm, poke holes all over the top of the cake using a skewer or fork.
    - Drizzle the honey glaze evenly over the top of the cake, allowing it to soak in.
6. **Garnish (optional):**
    - Garnish the cake with sliced almonds or chopped nuts, and arrange fresh eucalyptus leaves around the cake for decoration.
7. **Serve and enjoy:**
    - Slice and serve the eucalyptus honey cake. Enjoy the unique flavor of eucalyptus honey in this moist and fragrant dessert!

This eucalyptus honey cake is perfect for tea time or as a special treat for those who appreciate the distinct taste of eucalyptus honey. It's a delightful way to showcase this unique Australian ingredient in a delicious dessert.

Bush tomato cake

Ingredients:

- 1 cup dried bush tomatoes (kutjera)
- 1 cup boiling water
- 1 cup brown sugar
- 125g (1/2 cup) butter, softened
- 2 eggs
- 1 3/4 cups self-raising flour
- 1/2 cup milk
- 1 teaspoon vanilla extract
- Pinch of salt

Instructions:

1. **Prepare the Bush Tomatoes:**
    - Place the dried bush tomatoes in a heatproof bowl.
    - Pour the boiling water over them and let them soak for about 20 minutes to rehydrate.
    - Once softened, drain the bush tomatoes and roughly chop them. Set aside.
2. **Preheat Oven and Prepare Pan:**
    - Preheat your oven to 180°C (350°F).
    - Grease and line a 20cm (8-inch) round cake pan with baking paper.
3. **Make the Cake Batter:**
    - In a mixing bowl, cream together the softened butter and brown sugar until light and fluffy.
    - Add the eggs, one at a time, beating well after each addition.
    - Stir in the vanilla extract.
4. **Combine Dry Ingredients:**
    - Sift the self-raising flour and salt together.
5. **Alternate Mixing:**
    - Gradually add the flour mixture and milk to the butter-sugar mixture, starting and ending with the flour.
    - Mix until just combined.
6. **Fold in Bush Tomatoes:**
    - Gently fold in the chopped bush tomatoes until evenly distributed throughout the batter.
7. **Bake the Cake:**
    - Pour the batter into the prepared cake pan and smooth the top with a spatula.
    - Bake in the preheated oven for 40-45 minutes, or until a skewer inserted into the center comes out clean.
8. **Cool and Serve:**

- Allow the cake to cool in the pan for 10 minutes, then transfer to a wire rack to cool completely.
- Once cooled, slice and serve the bush tomato cake either plain or with a dollop of cream or ice cream.

Notes:

- **Bush Tomatoes:** Ensure the dried bush tomatoes are well rehydrated before chopping and incorporating them into the cake batter. They add a unique tangy flavor to the cake.
- **Texture:** This cake typically has a moist texture due to the addition of milk and butter. Ensure not to overmix the batter to keep it light.
- **Variations:** Some recipes may include additional spices such as cinnamon or nutmeg for added flavor complexity.

Bush tomato cake is a wonderful example of using indigenous Australian ingredients to create a delicious and distinctive dessert. Enjoy experimenting with this recipe and adjusting it to your taste preferences!

Tasmanian apple cake

Ingredients:

- 3-4 medium-sized apples (about 500g), peeled, cored, and thinly sliced
- 2 cups self-raising flour
- 1 teaspoon ground cinnamon
- 1/2 teaspoon ground nutmeg
- 1/2 teaspoon salt
- 200g unsalted butter, softened
- 1 cup caster sugar (superfine sugar)
- 3 eggs
- 1 teaspoon vanilla extract
- 1/2 cup milk
- 1/4 cup flaked almonds (optional, for topping)

Instructions:

1. **Preheat Oven and Prepare Pan:**
    - Preheat your oven to 180°C (350°F).
    - Grease and line a 20cm (8-inch) round cake pan with baking paper.
2. **Prepare the Apples:**
    - Peel, core, and thinly slice the apples. Set aside.
3. **Mix Dry Ingredients:**
    - In a medium bowl, sift together the self-raising flour, ground cinnamon, ground nutmeg, and salt. Set aside.
4. **Cream Butter and Sugar:**
    - In a large mixing bowl, cream together the softened butter and caster sugar until light and fluffy.
5. **Add Eggs and Vanilla:**
    - Add the eggs, one at a time, beating well after each addition.
    - Stir in the vanilla extract.
6. **Combine Wet and Dry Ingredients:**
    - Gradually add the flour mixture to the creamed butter and sugar, alternating with the milk, starting and ending with the flour mixture. Mix until just combined.
7. **Fold in Apples:**
    - Gently fold in the sliced apples until evenly distributed throughout the batter.
8. **Bake the Cake:**
    - Pour the batter into the prepared cake pan and smooth the top with a spatula.
    - Sprinkle the flaked almonds evenly over the top of the batter, if using.
9. **Bake and Serve:**
    - Bake in the preheated oven for 50-60 minutes, or until a skewer inserted into the center comes out clean.
10. **Cool and Enjoy:**

- Allow the cake to cool in the pan for 10 minutes, then transfer to a wire rack to cool completely.
- Once cooled, slice and serve the Tasmanian apple cake on its own or with a dusting of icing sugar or a dollop of cream.

Notes:

- **Apples:** Use fresh, crisp apples such as Granny Smith, Pink Lady, or Fuji for the best flavor and texture.
- **Variations:** You can add a handful of raisins or chopped nuts to the batter for added texture and flavor.
- **Storage:** Store any leftover cake in an airtight container at room temperature for up to 3 days, or refrigerate for longer freshness.

This Tasmanian apple cake is perfect for afternoon tea or as a delightful dessert, highlighting the natural sweetness of Tasmanian apples in a moist and flavorful cake. Enjoy baking and savoring this delicious treat!

Pumpkin and ginger cake

Ingredients:

- 1 cup cooked and mashed pumpkin (canned pumpkin puree can also be used)
- 1/2 cup unsalted butter, melted
- 1/2 cup brown sugar
- 1/2 cup granulated sugar
- 2 eggs
- 1 teaspoon vanilla extract
- 2 cups all-purpose flour
- 2 teaspoons baking powder
- 1 teaspoon ground cinnamon
- 1/2 teaspoon ground ginger
- 1/4 teaspoon ground nutmeg
- 1/4 teaspoon ground cloves
- 1/2 teaspoon salt
- 1/2 cup milk

Optional Ginger Glaze:

- 1 cup powdered sugar
- 1-2 tablespoons milk or cream
- 1/2 teaspoon ground ginger

Instructions:

1. **Preheat Oven and Prepare Pan:**
    - Preheat your oven to 180°C (350°F).
    - Grease and flour a 9-inch round cake pan or line it with parchment paper.
2. **Mix Wet Ingredients:**
    - In a large mixing bowl, combine the melted butter, brown sugar, and granulated sugar. Mix until well combined and smooth.
3. **Add Eggs and Vanilla:**
    - Beat in the eggs, one at a time, until fully incorporated.
    - Stir in the vanilla extract.
4. **Incorporate Pumpkin:**
    - Add the mashed pumpkin to the wet ingredients and mix until smooth and well combined.
5. **Combine Dry Ingredients:**
    - In a separate bowl, sift together the flour, baking powder, ground cinnamon, ground ginger, ground nutmeg, ground cloves, and salt.
6. **Combine Wet and Dry Mixtures:**

- Gradually add the dry ingredients to the pumpkin mixture, alternating with the milk, starting and ending with the dry ingredients. Mix until just combined. Be careful not to overmix.

7. **Bake the Cake:**
   - Pour the batter into the prepared cake pan and smooth the top with a spatula.
   - Bake in the preheated oven for 35-40 minutes, or until a toothpick inserted into the center comes out clean.

8. **Cool and Glaze (optional):**
   - Allow the cake to cool in the pan for 10 minutes, then transfer it to a wire rack to cool completely.
   - If desired, prepare the ginger glaze by whisking together powdered sugar, milk or cream, and ground ginger until smooth. Drizzle the glaze over the cooled cake.

9. **Serve and Enjoy:**
   - Slice and serve the pumpkin and ginger cake at room temperature. It pairs well with a cup of tea or coffee.

Notes:

- **Pumpkin:** You can use fresh cooked and mashed pumpkin or canned pumpkin puree. Make sure to drain any excess liquid from the pumpkin puree if using canned.
- **Spices:** Adjust the amount of ground ginger, cinnamon, nutmeg, and cloves to suit your taste preferences.
- **Storage:** Store leftover cake in an airtight container at room temperature for up to 3 days, or refrigerate for longer freshness.

This pumpkin and ginger cake is moist, flavorful, and perfect for any occasion, offering a wonderful blend of seasonal flavors. Enjoy baking and savoring this delicious treat!

Salted caramel mud cake

Ingredients:

For the Cake:

- 200g unsalted butter, chopped
- 200g good quality dark chocolate, chopped
- 1 cup (240ml) milk
- 1 cup (220g) brown sugar
- 1 cup (220g) caster sugar (superfine sugar)
- 2 teaspoons vanilla extract
- 2 large eggs, lightly beaten
- 1 3/4 cups (260g) plain flour
- 1/4 cup (30g) cocoa powder
- 1 teaspoon baking powder
- 1/2 teaspoon salt

For the Salted Caramel Sauce:

- 1 cup (220g) caster sugar (superfine sugar)
- 120g unsalted butter, cubed
- 1/2 cup (120ml) thickened cream (heavy cream)
- 1 teaspoon sea salt flakes (adjust to taste)

For the Salted Caramel Buttercream (optional):

- 200g unsalted butter, softened
- 2 cups (320g) icing sugar (powdered sugar)
- 1/2 cup salted caramel sauce (cooled)

Instructions:

1. Make the Salted Caramel Sauce:

- In a medium saucepan, heat the caster sugar over medium-high heat, stirring constantly with a wooden spoon.
- The sugar will form clumps and then melt into a thick amber-colored liquid as you continue to stir.
- Once the sugar is completely melted, immediately add the cubed butter. Be careful as the mixture will bubble rapidly.
- Stir the butter into the caramel until it is completely melted, about 2-3 minutes.
- Slowly drizzle in the cream while stirring. The mixture will bubble again.
- Allow the caramel to boil for 1 minute, then remove from heat and stir in the sea salt flakes.

- Set aside to cool. The caramel will thicken as it cools.

2. Make the Cake:

- Preheat your oven to 160°C (320°F). Grease and line a 9-inch (23cm) round cake pan with baking paper.
- In a large saucepan, combine the butter, dark chocolate, milk, brown sugar, and caster sugar over low heat. Stir until melted and smooth.
- Remove from heat and stir in the vanilla extract. Allow to cool slightly.
- Whisk in the lightly beaten eggs until well combined.
- Sift the flour, cocoa powder, baking powder, and salt over the chocolate mixture. Stir until just combined and no lumps remain.
- Pour the batter into the prepared cake pan and smooth the top with a spatula.
- Bake for 50-60 minutes, or until a skewer inserted into the center comes out with moist crumbs (not wet batter).
- Allow the cake to cool in the pan for 10 minutes, then transfer to a wire rack to cool completely.

3. Make the Salted Caramel Buttercream (optional):

- In a mixing bowl, beat the softened butter until creamy and smooth.
- Gradually add the icing sugar, beating well after each addition until light and fluffy.
- Beat in the cooled salted caramel sauce until well combined and smooth.

4. Assemble the Cake:

- Once the cake is completely cooled, you can choose to frost it with the salted caramel buttercream if desired. Spread the buttercream evenly over the top and sides of the cake.
- Drizzle extra salted caramel sauce over the top of the cake for decoration, allowing some to drip down the sides.
- Slice and serve the salted caramel mud cake at room temperature. Enjoy the rich caramel flavors and moist cake texture!

Notes:

- **Salted Caramel Sauce:** You can make the salted caramel sauce ahead of time and store it in the refrigerator. Warm it slightly before using to make it easier to drizzle over the cake.
- **Storage:** Store the cake in an airtight container at room temperature for up to 3 days. If frosted, store in the refrigerator and bring to room temperature before serving.
- **Variations:** For an extra touch, sprinkle a bit of additional sea salt flakes on top of the cake just before serving to enhance the salted caramel flavor.

This salted caramel mud cake is sure to impress with its rich, indulgent flavors. Enjoy baking and sharing this delicious dessert with family and friends!

Raspberry and white chocolate mud cake

Ingredients:

For the Cake:

- 200g white chocolate, chopped
- 200g unsalted butter, chopped
- 1 cup (240ml) milk
- 1 cup (220g) caster sugar (superfine sugar)
- 1 teaspoon vanilla extract
- 2 large eggs, lightly beaten
- 1 3/4 cups (260g) plain flour
- 1/2 cup (60g) almond meal (optional, for extra texture)
- 1 teaspoon baking powder
- 1/2 teaspoon salt
- 150g fresh raspberries (or frozen, thawed and drained)

For the White Chocolate Ganache:

- 200g white chocolate, finely chopped
- 1/2 cup (120ml) thickened cream (heavy cream)

For Decoration (optional):

- Fresh raspberries
- White chocolate curls or shavings

Instructions:

1. Prepare the Cake:

- Preheat your oven to 160°C (320°F). Grease and line a 9-inch (23cm) round cake pan with baking paper.
- In a saucepan over low heat, combine the chopped white chocolate, butter, milk, caster sugar, and vanilla extract. Stir continuously until melted and smooth. Remove from heat and allow to cool slightly.
- Whisk in the lightly beaten eggs until well combined.
- Sift the plain flour, almond meal (if using), baking powder, and salt into the chocolate mixture. Stir until smooth and no lumps remain.
- Gently fold in the raspberries, taking care not to crush them too much.
- Pour the batter into the prepared cake pan and smooth the top with a spatula.
- Bake for 50-60 minutes, or until a skewer inserted into the center comes out with moist crumbs (not wet batter).

- Allow the cake to cool in the pan for 10 minutes, then transfer to a wire rack to cool completely.

2. Make the White Chocolate Ganache:

- Place the finely chopped white chocolate in a heatproof bowl.
- In a small saucepan, heat the thickened cream over medium heat until it just begins to boil.
- Pour the hot cream over the chopped white chocolate. Let it sit for 1-2 minutes, then stir gently until smooth and well combined.
- Allow the ganache to cool and thicken slightly before using.

3. Assemble the Cake:

- Once the cake has cooled completely, pour the white chocolate ganache over the top of the cake, allowing it to drip down the sides.
- Use a spatula or knife to spread the ganache evenly over the top and sides of the cake.
- Decorate with fresh raspberries and white chocolate curls or shavings, if desired.

4. Serve and Enjoy:

- Slice and serve the raspberry and white chocolate mud cake at room temperature. Enjoy the delightful combination of raspberries and white chocolate in every bite!

Notes:

- **Raspberries:** Fresh raspberries work best for this cake, but you can use thawed and drained frozen raspberries if fresh ones are not available.
- **Almond Meal:** Adding almond meal enhances the texture of the cake, but you can omit it if preferred.
- **Storage:** Store the cake in an airtight container at room temperature for up to 3 days. If frosted with ganache, store in the refrigerator and bring to room temperature before serving.

This raspberry and white chocolate mud cake is perfect for special occasions or as a decadent treat for dessert lovers. Enjoy baking and sharing this delicious cake with friends and family!

Lemon cheesecake

Ingredients:

For the Crust:

- 200g digestive biscuits (graham crackers), crushed into fine crumbs
- 100g unsalted butter, melted

For the Cheesecake Filling:

- 500g cream cheese, softened (at room temperature)
- 200g granulated sugar
- Zest of 2 lemons
- 3 large eggs
- 1 teaspoon vanilla extract
- 1/2 cup (120ml) sour cream
- 1/4 cup (60ml) freshly squeezed lemon juice

For the Lemon Curd (optional topping):

- 1/2 cup (120ml) freshly squeezed lemon juice
- Zest of 1 lemon
- 1/2 cup (100g) granulated sugar
- 2 large eggs
- 3 tablespoons unsalted butter, cubed

Instructions:

1. Preheat Oven and Prepare Pan:

- Preheat your oven to 160°C (325°F). Grease a 9-inch (23cm) springform pan and line the bottom with parchment paper.

2. Make the Crust:

- In a bowl, mix together the crushed digestive biscuits and melted butter until well combined.
- Press the mixture firmly and evenly into the bottom of the prepared springform pan. Use the back of a spoon or a flat-bottomed glass to ensure it's packed tightly.
- Chill the crust in the refrigerator while preparing the filling.

3. Make the Cheesecake Filling:

- In a large mixing bowl, beat the softened cream cheese until smooth using an electric mixer.

- Add the granulated sugar and lemon zest, and beat until creamy and well combined.
- Add the eggs, one at a time, mixing well after each addition.
- Stir in the vanilla extract, sour cream, and freshly squeezed lemon juice until the mixture is smooth and creamy.

4. Assemble and Bake:

- Pour the cheesecake filling over the chilled crust in the springform pan.
- Tap the pan gently on the counter to release any air bubbles.
- Place the springform pan on a baking sheet and bake in the preheated oven for 45-50 minutes, or until the edges are set and the center is slightly jiggly.
- Turn off the oven and leave the cheesecake in the oven with the door slightly ajar for 1 hour to cool gradually.

5. Make the Lemon Curd (optional):

- In a small saucepan, whisk together the lemon juice, lemon zest, granulated sugar, and eggs.
- Cook over medium heat, stirring constantly, until the mixture thickens and coats the back of a spoon (about 5-7 minutes).
- Remove from heat and stir in the cubed butter until smooth.
- Strain the lemon curd through a fine-mesh sieve into a bowl. Cover with plastic wrap directly on the surface of the curd to prevent a skin from forming. Chill in the refrigerator until ready to use.

6. Chill and Serve:

- Once the cheesecake has cooled to room temperature, refrigerate for at least 4 hours, preferably overnight, until fully set.
- To serve, run a knife around the edge of the springform pan to loosen the cheesecake. Remove the sides of the pan.
- If using, spread the chilled lemon curd over the top of the cheesecake just before serving.
- Slice and serve the lemon cheesecake chilled. Enjoy the creamy texture and refreshing lemon flavor!

Notes:

- **Room Temperature Ingredients:** Ensure the cream cheese is softened at room temperature to avoid lumps in the cheesecake batter.
- **Chilling Time:** Allowing the cheesecake to chill thoroughly ensures it sets properly and achieves the perfect texture.
- **Variations:** You can add a tablespoon of lemon zest into the cheesecake batter for extra lemon flavor, or garnish with whipped cream and fresh berries for added decoration.

This lemon cheesecake is a wonderful dessert for any occasion, with its creamy texture and bright lemony taste. Enjoy making and savoring this delightful treat!

Chocolate ripple cake

Ingredients:

- 1 packet (about 250g) Arnott's chocolate ripple biscuits (or similar chocolate wafers)
- 600ml thickened cream (heavy cream), chilled
- 1 teaspoon vanilla extract
- 2 tablespoons icing sugar (powdered sugar), optional
- Grated chocolate or cocoa powder, for garnish (optional)

Instructions:

1. **Prepare the Cream:**
   - In a large mixing bowl, combine the chilled thickened cream, vanilla extract, and icing sugar (if using).
   - Whip the cream using an electric mixer or a whisk until stiff peaks form. The cream should be thick enough to spread easily but not over-whipped.
2. **Assemble the Cake:**
   - On a serving plate or cake stand, place one chocolate ripple biscuit flat.
   - Spread a thin layer of whipped cream evenly over the biscuit.
   - Place another biscuit on top and press gently to adhere.
   - Repeat this process, layering biscuits with whipped cream, until you have used all the biscuits. You can stack them in a log shape or create a round cake shape, depending on your preference.
3. **Frost and Decorate:**
   - Once all biscuits are stacked and covered with whipped cream, use the remaining cream to frost the entire cake evenly.
   - Smooth the sides and top of the cake with a spatula for a neat finish.
4. **Chill Overnight:**
   - Cover the cake with plastic wrap or place it in an airtight container.
   - Refrigerate overnight or for at least 6 hours. This allows the biscuits to soften and absorb moisture from the cream, creating a cake-like texture.
5. **Serve:**
   - Before serving, garnish the chocolate ripple cake with grated chocolate or a dusting of cocoa powder if desired.
   - Slice the cake using a sharp knife and serve chilled.

Tips:

- **Variations:** You can add a layer of fruit (such as berries) or sprinkle crushed nuts between the layers for added texture and flavor.
- **Decoration:** Get creative with your decorations; some like to drizzle chocolate sauce over the top or add fresh berries for a pop of color.

- **Storage:** Store any leftovers in the refrigerator for up to 2-3 days. The cake will continue to soften and develop flavor.

Chocolate ripple cake is perfect for summer gatherings, potlucks, or any occasion where you want to serve a delicious, fuss-free dessert. Enjoy making this simple yet delightful treat!

Bush tucker fruitcake

Ingredients:

- 1 cup dried bush tomatoes (kutjera), chopped
- 1 cup dried quandongs, chopped (wild peach)
- 1/2 cup dried riberry (lilli pilli), chopped
- 1/2 cup dried Davidson's plum, chopped
- 1/2 cup dried bush raisins (muntries), chopped
- 1/2 cup dried wild rosella flowers, chopped
- 1/2 cup macadamia nuts, chopped
- 1/2 cup dried figs, chopped
- 1/2 cup dried dates, chopped
- 1/2 cup dried apricots, chopped
- 1/2 cup dried cherries
- 1/2 cup dried blueberries
- Zest and juice of 1 orange
- Zest and juice of 1 lemon
- 1/2 cup rum or brandy (optional)
- 250g unsalted butter, softened
- 1 cup brown sugar
- 4 large eggs
- 1 1/2 cups plain flour
- 1/2 cup almond meal
- 1 teaspoon baking powder
- 1 teaspoon ground cinnamon
- 1/2 teaspoon ground nutmeg
- 1/2 teaspoon ground ginger
- 1/4 teaspoon ground cloves
- 1/2 teaspoon salt

Instructions:

1. **Prepare the Fruit and Nuts:**
   - In a large bowl, combine all the dried bush tucker fruits, nuts, and berries: bush tomatoes, quandongs, riberry, Davidson's plum, bush raisins, wild rosella flowers, macadamia nuts, figs, dates, apricots, cherries, and blueberries.
   - Add the orange zest and juice, lemon zest and juice, and rum or brandy (if using). Mix well to combine. Let the mixture soak for at least 1 hour, preferably overnight, to allow the flavors to meld.
2. **Preheat Oven and Prepare Pan:**
   - Preheat your oven to 160°C (320°F). Grease and line a 22cm (9-inch) round cake pan with baking paper.
3. **Make the Cake Batter:**

- In a separate large mixing bowl, cream together the softened butter and brown sugar until light and fluffy.
- Add the eggs, one at a time, beating well after each addition.
- In another bowl, sift together the plain flour, almond meal, baking powder, ground cinnamon, ground nutmeg, ground ginger, ground cloves, and salt.

4. **Combine Wet and Dry Mixtures:**
   - Gradually add the dry ingredients to the butter-sugar mixture, alternating with the soaked fruit and nut mixture. Start and end with the flour mixture. Mix until just combined. Do not overmix.

5. **Bake the Cake:**
   - Pour the batter into the prepared cake pan and smooth the top with a spatula.
   - Bake in the preheated oven for 1 1/2 to 2 hours, or until a skewer inserted into the center comes out clean. If the top of the cake begins to brown too quickly, cover loosely with foil.

6. **Cool and Serve:**
   - Allow the cake to cool in the pan for 10-15 minutes, then transfer to a wire rack to cool completely.

7. **Storage:**
   - Once cooled, store the bush tucker fruitcake in an airtight container at room temperature. For best flavor, allow the cake to mature for a few days before serving.

Notes:

- **Bush Tucker Ingredients:** Adjust the quantities and types of bush tucker fruits and nuts according to availability and personal preference. These ingredients can usually be found at specialty stores or online suppliers.
- **Alcohol:** The rum or brandy is optional but adds richness to the flavor of the cake. If preferred, you can omit it or substitute with orange juice.
- **Decoration:** You can decorate the cake with a dusting of icing sugar, or glaze with a simple syrup or melted apricot jam for a glossy finish.

This bush tucker fruitcake celebrates the unique flavors of Australia's native ingredients, making it a special and memorable dessert for any occasion. Enjoy the rich, fruity flavors and textures of this delightful cake!

Meringue roulade

Ingredients:

For the Meringue:

- 4 large egg whites, at room temperature
- 200g (1 cup) caster sugar (superfine sugar)
- 1 teaspoon cornstarch (cornflour)
- 1 teaspoon white vinegar
- 1 teaspoon vanilla extract

For the Filling:

- 300ml (1 1/4 cups) double cream (heavy cream)
- 2 tablespoons icing sugar (powdered sugar)
- 1 teaspoon vanilla extract
- Fresh berries or fruit compote for filling (optional)

Instructions:

1. Preheat Oven and Prepare Baking Sheet:

- Preheat your oven to 180°C (350°F). Line a large baking sheet (approximately 30x40cm or 12x16 inches) with parchment paper.

2. Make the Meringue:

- In a clean, dry mixing bowl, beat the egg whites with an electric mixer on medium-high speed until soft peaks form.
- Gradually add the caster sugar, a spoonful at a time, while continuing to beat the egg whites. Beat until stiff peaks form and the meringue is glossy.
- Sprinkle the cornstarch, white vinegar, and vanilla extract over the meringue, and gently fold them in using a spatula. Be careful not to deflate the meringue.

3. Spread and Bake the Meringue:

- Spoon the meringue onto the prepared baking sheet and spread it out evenly into a rectangle shape, about 1cm (1/2 inch) thick.

4. Bake the Meringue:

- Place the baking sheet in the preheated oven and immediately reduce the temperature to 150°C (300°F). Bake for 25-30 minutes, or until the meringue is firm to the touch and lightly golden on top.

5. Prepare the Filling:

- While the meringue is baking, prepare the filling. In a mixing bowl, whip the double cream with icing sugar and vanilla extract until stiff peaks form.

6. Assemble the Roulade:

- Remove the baked meringue from the oven and let it cool in the baking sheet for a few minutes.
- Lay a clean tea towel or parchment paper on a work surface and dust lightly with icing sugar.
- Carefully invert the warm meringue onto the tea towel or parchment paper.
- Peel off the parchment paper from the bottom of the meringue.

7. Fill and Roll the Roulade:

- Spread the whipped cream evenly over the surface of the meringue, leaving a small border around the edges.
- If desired, add fresh berries or a fruit compote evenly over the cream.
- Using the tea towel or parchment paper as a guide, roll up the meringue from one of the shorter ends, lifting and rolling gently but firmly.

8. Chill and Serve:

- Transfer the rolled meringue roulade onto a serving platter, seam side down.
- Chill in the refrigerator for at least 1 hour before serving to allow the filling to set.
- Slice and serve the meringue roulade chilled. Dust with icing sugar and garnish with additional berries if desired.

Tips:

- **Beating Egg Whites:** Ensure your mixing bowl and beaters are clean and free of any grease, as any trace of fat can prevent the egg whites from whipping up properly.
- **Filling Variations:** You can customize the filling with different flavors such as lemon curd, chocolate ganache, or different types of fresh fruit.
- **Handling the Meringue:** When rolling the meringue, work gently but confidently to avoid cracking. The meringue is delicate but should hold its shape well if handled carefully.

This meringue roulade makes for an elegant dessert, perfect for special occasions or gatherings. It's light, airy, and offers a delightful combination of textures and flavors. Enjoy making and serving this beautiful dessert!

Peach Melba cake

Ingredients:

For the Cake:

- 1 cup unsalted butter, softened
- 1 cup granulated sugar
- 4 large eggs
- 2 teaspoons vanilla extract
- 2 cups all-purpose flour
- 2 teaspoons baking powder
- 1/2 teaspoon salt
- 1/2 cup milk

For the Peach Filling:

- 2 cups fresh or canned peach slices (drained if canned)
- 2 tablespoons granulated sugar
- 1 tablespoon lemon juice

For the Raspberry Sauce:

- 1 cup fresh or frozen raspberries
- 2 tablespoons granulated sugar
- 1 tablespoon lemon juice

For the Vanilla Buttercream:

- 1 cup unsalted butter, softened
- 4 cups icing sugar (powdered sugar)
- 2 teaspoons vanilla extract
- 2-4 tablespoons milk or cream

For Garnish:

- Fresh raspberries
- Fresh peach slices

Instructions:

1. Make the Cake:

- Preheat your oven to 180°C (350°F). Grease and flour two 9-inch round cake pans.
- In a large mixing bowl, cream together the softened butter and granulated sugar until light and fluffy.

- Add the eggs one at a time, beating well after each addition. Stir in the vanilla extract.
- In another bowl, sift together the flour, baking powder, and salt.
- Gradually add the dry ingredients to the butter mixture, alternating with the milk. Begin and end with the dry ingredients. Mix until just combined.
- Divide the batter evenly between the prepared cake pans and smooth the tops with a spatula.
- Bake for 25-30 minutes, or until a toothpick inserted into the center of the cakes comes out clean.
- Remove from the oven and let the cakes cool in the pans for 10 minutes before transferring them to wire racks to cool completely.

2. Prepare the Peach Filling:

- In a saucepan, combine the peach slices, granulated sugar, and lemon juice.
- Cook over medium heat, stirring occasionally, until the peaches are tender and the sugar has dissolved, about 5-7 minutes.
- Remove from heat and let cool completely.

3. Make the Raspberry Sauce:

- In a blender or food processor, puree the raspberries, granulated sugar, and lemon juice until smooth.
- Strain the raspberry mixture through a fine-mesh sieve into a bowl to remove the seeds. Discard the seeds.
- Chill the raspberry sauce in the refrigerator until ready to use.

4. Prepare the Vanilla Buttercream:

- In a large mixing bowl, beat the softened butter until creamy.
- Gradually add the icing sugar, 1 cup at a time, beating well after each addition.
- Add the vanilla extract and 2 tablespoons of milk or cream. Beat until smooth and fluffy, adding more milk or cream if needed to achieve a spreadable consistency.

5. Assemble the Cake:

- Place one cake layer on a serving plate or cake stand.
- Spread a layer of vanilla buttercream over the top of the cake layer.
- Spoon half of the peach filling over the buttercream and spread evenly.
- Place the second cake layer on top and gently press down.
- Frost the top and sides of the cake with the remaining vanilla buttercream.
- Drizzle the raspberry sauce over the top of the cake, allowing it to drip down the sides.
- Garnish with fresh raspberries and peach slices.

6. Chill and Serve:

- Refrigerate the Peach Melba cake for at least 1 hour to allow the flavors to meld and the buttercream to set.
- Slice and serve chilled. Enjoy the delicious combination of peach, raspberry, and vanilla flavors!

Notes:

- **Variations:** You can adjust the sweetness of the raspberry sauce and peach filling according to your taste. If fresh peaches are not available, canned peaches (drained) can be used.
- **Storage:** Store any leftover cake in an airtight container in the refrigerator for up to 3 days.

This Peach Melba cake is a delightful dessert that captures the essence of the classic Peach Melba flavors in a beautiful and delicious cake form. It's perfect for special occasions or anytime you want to impress with a stunning dessert!

Cherry ripe cheesecake

Ingredients:

For the Base:

- 200g digestive biscuits (graham crackers), crushed
- 100g unsalted butter, melted

For the Cheesecake Filling:

- 500g cream cheese, softened
- 200g caster sugar (superfine sugar)
- 1 teaspoon vanilla extract
- 200ml thickened cream (heavy cream)
- 200g dark chocolate, melted and cooled slightly
- 1 cup desiccated coconut
- 1 cup glace cherries, chopped
- 100g dark chocolate, chopped (for decoration)

For the Topping:

- 200ml thickened cream (heavy cream)
- 200g dark chocolate, chopped

Instructions:

1. Prepare the Base:

- Grease a 9-inch (23cm) springform pan and line the bottom with parchment paper.
- In a bowl, mix together the crushed digestive biscuits and melted butter until well combined.
- Press the mixture firmly and evenly into the bottom of the prepared pan. Use the back of a spoon or a flat-bottomed glass to ensure it's packed tightly.
- Chill in the refrigerator while preparing the filling.

2. Make the Cheesecake Filling:

- In a large mixing bowl, beat the softened cream cheese, caster sugar, and vanilla extract until smooth and creamy.
- Add the thickened cream and beat until the mixture is thick and holds its shape.
- Fold in the melted dark chocolate, desiccated coconut, and chopped glace cherries until evenly distributed.

3. Assemble the Cheesecake:

- Pour the cheesecake filling over the prepared biscuit base in the springform pan. Smooth the top with a spatula.
- Chill in the refrigerator for at least 4 hours, preferably overnight, to set.

4. Make the Topping:

- In a small saucepan, heat the thickened cream until it just begins to boil.
- Remove from heat and add the chopped dark chocolate. Let it sit for 1-2 minutes, then stir gently until smooth and well combined.
- Allow the ganache to cool and thicken slightly before pouring over the chilled cheesecake.

5. Decorate and Serve:

- Pour the chocolate ganache over the top of the chilled cheesecake, spreading it evenly with a spatula.
- Sprinkle with additional chopped dark chocolate for decoration, if desired.
- Return the cheesecake to the refrigerator to set the ganache for at least 1 hour.

6. Serve and Enjoy:

- Once the ganache is set, carefully remove the sides of the springform pan.
- Slice and serve the Cherry Ripe cheesecake chilled.
- Enjoy the rich flavors of cherries, coconut, and dark chocolate in every bite!

Notes:

- **Glace Cherries:** If you prefer, you can substitute glace cherries with fresh cherries or cherry preserves for a slightly different texture and flavor.
- **Storage:** Store any leftover cheesecake in an airtight container in the refrigerator for up to 3-4 days.

This Cherry Ripe cheesecake is a luxurious and indulgent dessert that combines the beloved flavors of the Cherry Ripe chocolate bar into a creamy and delightful cheesecake. It's perfect for special occasions or whenever you crave a rich and satisfying treat!

Beetroot and chocolate cake

Ingredients:

For the Cake:

- 250g cooked beetroot (about 2-3 medium beetroots), peeled and grated
- 200g dark chocolate (at least 70% cocoa), chopped
- 200g unsalted butter, diced
- 200g caster sugar (superfine sugar)
- 4 large eggs
- 1 teaspoon vanilla extract
- 150g plain flour
- 50g cocoa powder
- 2 teaspoons baking powder
- Pinch of salt

For the Chocolate Ganache (optional):

- 150g dark chocolate, chopped
- 150ml double cream (heavy cream)

For Garnish (optional):

- Fresh berries
- Icing sugar (powdered sugar)

Instructions:

1. Prepare the Beetroot:

- Preheat your oven to 180°C (350°F). Grease and line a 9-inch (23cm) round cake pan with parchment paper.
- Cook the beetroots until tender (you can boil, steam, or roast them). Once cooled, peel and grate them finely. Set aside.

2. Make the Cake:

- In a heatproof bowl, combine the chopped dark chocolate and diced butter. Melt together gently over a pan of simmering water (double boiler), stirring occasionally until smooth. Remove from heat and let it cool slightly.
- In a large mixing bowl, whisk together the caster sugar, eggs, and vanilla extract until pale and fluffy.
- Gradually fold in the melted chocolate and butter mixture into the egg mixture until well combined.

- Sift in the plain flour, cocoa powder, baking powder, and salt. Fold gently until just combined.
- Finally, fold in the grated beetroot until evenly distributed throughout the batter.
- Pour the batter into the prepared cake pan and smooth the top with a spatula.

3. Bake the Cake:

- Bake in the preheated oven for 40-45 minutes, or until a skewer inserted into the center comes out clean.
- Remove from the oven and let the cake cool in the pan for 10 minutes, then transfer to a wire rack to cool completely.

4. Make the Chocolate Ganache (optional):

- In a small saucepan, heat the double cream until it just begins to boil.
- Remove from heat and add the chopped dark chocolate. Let it sit for 1-2 minutes, then stir gently until smooth and well combined.
- Let the ganache cool and thicken slightly before spreading over the cooled cake.

5. Serve and Garnish:

- Once the cake and ganache are completely cooled, spread the ganache over the top of the cake.
- Garnish with fresh berries and dust with icing sugar if desired.
- Slice and serve the beetroot and chocolate cake at room temperature.

Notes:

- **Beetroot Preparation:** Make sure the cooked beetroot is cooled and well-drained before grating.
- **Chocolate:** Use good quality dark chocolate for both the cake and the ganache to enhance the richness of flavors.
- **Storage:** Store any leftover cake in an airtight container at room temperature for up to 3-4 days, or refrigerate for longer shelf life.

This beetroot and chocolate cake is a wonderful way to incorporate vegetables into a dessert while enjoying the deep, moist texture and rich chocolate flavor. It's a great choice for those looking to try something new and delicious!

Date and walnut cake

Ingredients:

For the Cake:

- 200g pitted dates, chopped
- 250ml water
- 1 teaspoon baking soda
- 150g unsalted butter, softened
- 150g brown sugar
- 2 large eggs
- 1 teaspoon vanilla extract
- 250g plain flour
- 1 teaspoon baking powder
- 1/2 teaspoon ground cinnamon
- 1/4 teaspoon ground nutmeg
- 100g walnuts, chopped

For the Topping (optional):

- 50g walnuts, chopped
- 2 tablespoons honey or maple syrup

Instructions:

1. Prepare the Dates:

- Preheat your oven to 180°C (350°F). Grease and line a 9-inch (23cm) round cake pan with parchment paper.
- In a saucepan, combine the chopped dates and water. Bring to a boil over medium heat.
- Remove from heat and stir in the baking soda. Let it sit for 5-10 minutes to soften the dates.

2. Make the Cake Batter:

- In a large mixing bowl, cream together the softened butter and brown sugar until light and fluffy.
- Add the eggs, one at a time, beating well after each addition. Stir in the vanilla extract.
- Sift in the plain flour, baking powder, ground cinnamon, and ground nutmeg. Mix until well combined.
- Fold in the softened date mixture and chopped walnuts until evenly distributed throughout the batter.

3. Bake the Cake:

- Pour the batter into the prepared cake pan and spread evenly with a spatula.
- Bake in the preheated oven for 35-40 minutes, or until a skewer inserted into the center comes out clean.
- Remove from the oven and let the cake cool in the pan for 10 minutes, then transfer to a wire rack to cool completely.

4. Optional Topping:

- If desired, while the cake is still warm, arrange the chopped walnuts on top and drizzle with honey or maple syrup for extra sweetness and decoration.

5. Serve and Enjoy:

- Once cooled, slice and serve the date and walnut cake at room temperature.
- Enjoy the moist and flavorful combination of dates and walnuts in every bite!

Notes:

- **Variations:** You can add a touch of orange zest or a splash of rum to the date mixture for added flavor.
- **Storage:** Store any leftover cake in an airtight container at room temperature for up to 3-4 days, or refrigerate for longer shelf life.

This date and walnut cake is perfect for afternoon tea or as a comforting dessert. It's easy to make and delivers a wonderful balance of sweetness and nuttiness that everyone will love.

Lamington cake

Ingredients:

For the Sponge Cake:

- 225g unsalted butter, softened
- 225g caster sugar (superfine sugar)
- 4 large eggs
- 1 teaspoon vanilla extract
- 300g self-raising flour
- Pinch of salt
- 120ml milk

For the Chocolate Icing:

- 300g icing sugar (powdered sugar)
- 75g cocoa powder
- 60g unsalted butter, melted
- 180ml milk
- 300g desiccated coconut, for coating

Instructions:

1. Prepare the Sponge Cake:

- Preheat your oven to 180°C (350°F). Grease and line a 20cm (8-inch) square cake tin with parchment paper.
- In a large mixing bowl, cream together the softened butter and caster sugar until pale and fluffy.
- Add the eggs, one at a time, beating well after each addition. Stir in the vanilla extract.
- Sift the self-raising flour and salt into the bowl. Fold gently into the mixture.
- Gradually add the milk, stirring until the batter is smooth and well combined.
- Pour the batter into the prepared cake tin and smooth the top with a spatula.
- Bake in the preheated oven for 25-30 minutes, or until a skewer inserted into the center comes out clean.
- Remove from the oven and let the cake cool in the tin for 10 minutes, then transfer to a wire rack to cool completely.

2. Prepare the Chocolate Icing:

- Sift the icing sugar and cocoa powder into a large bowl.
- Add the melted butter and milk, and stir until smooth and well combined. The icing should be thick enough to coat the cake without dripping off too quickly.

3. Assemble the Lamington Cake:

- Once the sponge cake is completely cooled, cut it into squares or desired shapes.
- Pour the desiccated coconut into a shallow bowl.
- Using a fork or a skewer, dip each square of cake into the chocolate icing, ensuring it is evenly coated on all sides.
- Allow any excess icing to drip off, then roll the coated cake in the desiccated coconut until well covered.
- Place the coated Lamington cake squares on a wire rack to set.

4. Serve and Enjoy:

- Once the chocolate icing has set, arrange the Lamington cake squares on a serving platter.
- Serve at room temperature and enjoy the delicious combination of chocolate, coconut, and sponge cake!

Notes:

- **Variations:** For a twist, you can add a layer of whipped cream and raspberry jam between two layers of sponge cake before coating with chocolate and coconut.
- **Storage:** Store any leftover Lamington cake in an airtight container at room temperature for up to 3-4 days.

This Lamington cake recipe brings together the iconic flavors of the traditional Lamington in a cake form, making it perfect for parties, afternoon tea, or whenever you crave a delightful and nostalgic treat.

Lemon curd cake

Ingredients:

For the Cake:

- 200g unsalted butter, softened
- 200g caster sugar (superfine sugar)
- 4 large eggs
- 1 teaspoon vanilla extract
- Zest of 2 lemons
- 200g self-raising flour
- 1 teaspoon baking powder
- 2-3 tablespoons milk (if needed)

For the Lemon Curd:

- 3-4 lemons, zest and juice (you will need about 150ml of lemon juice)
- 200g caster sugar (superfine sugar)
- 100g unsalted butter, cubed
- 4 large eggs, beaten

For the Lemon Buttercream Frosting:

- 250g unsalted butter, softened
- 500g icing sugar (powdered sugar), sifted
- Zest of 1-2 lemons
- 2-3 tablespoons lemon juice
- Yellow food coloring (optional, for color)

Instructions:

1. Make the Lemon Curd:

- In a heatproof bowl, whisk together the lemon zest, lemon juice, caster sugar, butter cubes, and beaten eggs.
- Place the bowl over a saucepan of simmering water (double boiler method), ensuring the bottom of the bowl does not touch the water.
- Whisk continuously until the mixture thickens and coats the back of a spoon, about 10-15 minutes.
- Remove from heat and let it cool. Once cooled, cover and refrigerate until ready to use.

2. Prepare the Cake:

- Preheat your oven to 180°C (350°F). Grease and line two 8-inch (20cm) round cake pans with parchment paper.

- In a large mixing bowl, cream together the softened butter and caster sugar until light and fluffy.
- Add the eggs, one at a time, beating well after each addition. Mix in the vanilla extract and lemon zest.
- Sift the self-raising flour and baking powder into the bowl. Fold gently into the mixture until just combined. If the batter is too thick, add 2-3 tablespoons of milk to loosen it slightly.
- Divide the batter evenly between the prepared cake pans and smooth the tops with a spatula.
- Bake in the preheated oven for 20-25 minutes, or until a skewer inserted into the center of the cakes comes out clean.
- Remove from the oven and let the cakes cool in the pans for 10 minutes, then transfer to a wire rack to cool completely.

3. Make the Lemon Buttercream Frosting:

- In a large mixing bowl, beat the softened butter until creamy and smooth.
- Gradually add the sifted icing sugar, one cup at a time, beating well after each addition.
- Mix in the lemon zest and lemon juice until the frosting is light and fluffy. Add a few drops of yellow food coloring if desired, to achieve a pale lemon color.

4. Assemble the Cake:

- Place one cooled cake layer on a serving plate or cake stand.
- Spread a layer of lemon curd over the top of the cake layer.
- Place the second cake layer on top, pressing gently to sandwich the layers together.
- Frost the top and sides of the cake with the lemon buttercream frosting, using a spatula to create smooth or textured swirls.

5. Serve and Enjoy:

- Slice and serve the lemon curd cake at room temperature.
- Store any leftover cake in an airtight container in the refrigerator. Bring to room temperature before serving for best flavor and texture.

Notes:

- **Lemon Curd:** You can make the lemon curd ahead of time and store it in the refrigerator for up to a week. It also makes a delicious spread for toast or scones!
- **Decoration:** Garnish the cake with additional lemon zest curls, fresh berries, or edible flowers for an elegant presentation.
- **Variations:** For a lighter option, you can use a whipped cream frosting instead of buttercream.

This Lemon Curd Cake is perfect for lemon lovers and makes a wonderful dessert for any occasion, from birthdays to afternoon tea gatherings. Enjoy the bright and zesty flavors of lemon in every slice!

Mint slice cake

Ingredients:

For the Chocolate Cake:

- 200g unsalted butter, softened
- 200g caster sugar (superfine sugar)
- 4 large eggs
- 1 teaspoon vanilla extract
- 200g self-raising flour
- 50g cocoa powder
- 1 teaspoon baking powder
- 2-3 tablespoons milk (if needed)

For the Mint Frosting:

- 200g unsalted butter, softened
- 400g icing sugar (powdered sugar), sifted
- 1-2 teaspoons peppermint extract (adjust to taste)
- Green food coloring (optional, for color)

For the Chocolate Ganache:

- 200g dark chocolate, chopped
- 200ml double cream (heavy cream)

For Decoration (optional):

- Mint chocolate biscuits (such as Arnott's Mint Slice), crushed
- Mint leaves
- Extra chocolate curls or shavings

Instructions:

1. Make the Chocolate Cake:

- Preheat your oven to 180°C (350°F). Grease and line two 8-inch (20cm) round cake pans with parchment paper.
- In a large mixing bowl, cream together the softened butter and caster sugar until light and fluffy.
- Add the eggs, one at a time, beating well after each addition. Mix in the vanilla extract.
- Sift the self-raising flour, cocoa powder, and baking powder into the bowl. Fold gently into the mixture until just combined. If the batter is too thick, add 2-3 tablespoons of milk to loosen it slightly.

- Divide the batter evenly between the prepared cake pans and smooth the tops with a spatula.
- Bake in the preheated oven for 20-25 minutes, or until a skewer inserted into the center of the cakes comes out clean.
- Remove from the oven and let the cakes cool in the pans for 10 minutes, then transfer to a wire rack to cool completely.

2. Make the Mint Frosting:

- In a large mixing bowl, beat the softened butter until creamy and smooth.
- Gradually add the sifted icing sugar, one cup at a time, beating well after each addition.
- Mix in the peppermint extract, adjusting to taste, and add green food coloring if desired to achieve a minty green color.

3. Assemble the Cake:

- Place one cooled cake layer on a serving plate or cake stand.
- Spread a layer of mint frosting evenly over the top of the cake layer.
- Place the second cake layer on top, pressing gently to sandwich the layers together.
- Frost the top and sides of the cake with the remaining mint frosting, using a spatula to create smooth or textured swirls.

4. Make the Chocolate Ganache:

- Place the chopped dark chocolate in a heatproof bowl.
- In a small saucepan, heat the double cream over medium heat until it just begins to simmer.
- Pour the hot cream over the chopped chocolate and let it sit for 1-2 minutes.
- Stir gently until smooth and well combined. Let the ganache cool and thicken slightly.

5. Decorate the Cake:

- Pour the chocolate ganache over the top of the frosted cake, allowing it to drip down the sides.
- Sprinkle crushed Mint Slice biscuits over the ganache while it's still soft.
- Garnish with mint leaves and chocolate curls or shavings for an elegant finish.

6. Serve and Enjoy:

- Chill the Mint Slice Cake in the refrigerator for about 30 minutes to set the ganache.
- Slice and serve the cake chilled or at room temperature.
- Enjoy the refreshing mint flavor and decadent chocolate layers!

Notes:

- **Mint Extract:** Adjust the amount of peppermint extract according to your taste preference. Start with a smaller amount and add more if you prefer a stronger mint flavor.
- **Storage:** Store any leftover cake in an airtight container in the refrigerator for up to 3-4 days.

This Mint Slice Cake is perfect for mint chocolate lovers and makes a stunning dessert for special occasions or celebrations. The combination of chocolate cake, mint frosting, and chocolate ganache creates a deliciously indulgent treat!

Black forest cake

Ingredients:

For the Chocolate Sponge Cake:

- 6 large eggs, at room temperature
- 200g caster sugar (superfine sugar)
- 150g plain flour
- 50g cocoa powder
- 1 teaspoon baking powder
- 1/4 teaspoon salt

For the Cherry Filling:

- 500g cherries (fresh or canned pitted cherries), drained (reserve some for decoration)
- 2-3 tablespoons Kirsch (cherry brandy), optional
- 2 tablespoons granulated sugar
- 1 tablespoon cornstarch (cornflour)
- 1 tablespoon water

For the Whipped Cream Frosting:

- 600ml double cream (heavy cream), chilled
- 3 tablespoons icing sugar (powdered sugar)
- 1 teaspoon vanilla extract

For Decoration:

- Chocolate shavings or curls
- Fresh cherries

Instructions:

1. Make the Chocolate Sponge Cake:

- Preheat your oven to 180°C (350°F). Grease and line two 8-inch (20cm) round cake pans with parchment paper.
- In a large mixing bowl, whisk together the eggs and caster sugar until pale and fluffy, about 5-7 minutes.
- In a separate bowl, sift together the plain flour, cocoa powder, baking powder, and salt.
- Gradually fold the dry ingredients into the egg mixture until just combined. Be gentle to avoid deflating the batter.
- Divide the batter evenly between the prepared cake pans and smooth the tops with a spatula.

- Bake in the preheated oven for 25-30 minutes, or until a skewer inserted into the center of the cakes comes out clean.
- Remove from the oven and let the cakes cool in the pans for 10 minutes, then transfer to a wire rack to cool completely.

2. Prepare the Cherry Filling:

- In a saucepan, combine the cherries (reserving some for decoration), Kirsch (if using), and granulated sugar.
- Cook over medium heat until the cherries release their juices and soften slightly, about 5-7 minutes.
- In a small bowl, mix the cornstarch with water to create a slurry. Stir the slurry into the cherry mixture and cook, stirring constantly, until the mixture thickens. Remove from heat and let it cool completely.

3. Make the Whipped Cream Frosting:

- In a large mixing bowl, beat the chilled double cream, icing sugar, and vanilla extract until stiff peaks form. Be careful not to over-whip.

4. Assemble the Black Forest Cake:

- Place one cooled cake layer on a serving plate or cake stand.
- Spread a layer of whipped cream frosting over the top of the cake layer.
- Spoon half of the cherry filling over the whipped cream, spreading evenly.
- Place the second cake layer on top and press gently to sandwich the layers together.
- Frost the top and sides of the cake with the remaining whipped cream frosting, creating swirls with a spatula.

5. Decorate the Cake:

- Use a spoon or piping bag to decorate the top of the cake with dollops of whipped cream.
- Garnish with chocolate shavings or curls around the sides and on top of the cake.
- Place reserved cherries on top for decoration.

6. Chill and Serve:

- Chill the Black Forest Cake in the refrigerator for at least 1 hour before serving to allow the flavors to meld and the frosting to set.
- Slice and serve chilled, and enjoy the rich and decadent flavors of chocolate, cherries, and cream!

Notes:

- **Kirsch:** Traditionally, Black Forest Cake is made with Kirsch (cherry brandy), which adds flavor to the cherries. You can omit it if preferred.
- **Storage:** Store any leftover cake in an airtight container in the refrigerator for up to 2-3 days.

This classic Black Forest Cake recipe is perfect for celebrations and special occasions, offering a delightful combination of chocolate, cherries, and creamy goodness that will impress your guests and satisfy any sweet tooth!

Blueberry and almond cake

Ingredients:

For the Cake:

- 150g unsalted butter, softened
- 150g caster sugar (superfine sugar)
- 3 large eggs
- 1 teaspoon almond extract
- 150g self-raising flour
- 100g ground almonds (almond meal)
- 100ml milk
- 150g fresh blueberries

For the Almond Streusel Topping:

- 50g plain flour
- 50g caster sugar (superfine sugar)
- 50g cold unsalted butter, cubed
- 50g flaked almonds

For Decoration (optional):

- Icing sugar (powdered sugar)
- Fresh blueberries

Instructions:

1. Preheat the Oven and Prepare the Pan:

- Preheat your oven to 180°C (350°F). Grease and line a 9-inch (23cm) round cake tin with parchment paper.

2. Make the Almond Streusel Topping:

- In a bowl, combine the plain flour and caster sugar.
- Rub in the cold cubed butter with your fingertips until the mixture resembles breadcrumbs.
- Stir in the flaked almonds. Set aside.

3. Prepare the Cake Batter:

- In a large mixing bowl, cream together the softened butter and caster sugar until light and fluffy.
- Add the eggs, one at a time, beating well after each addition. Mix in the almond extract.

- Fold in the self-raising flour and ground almonds until combined.
- Gradually add the milk, stirring until the batter is smooth and well combined.
- Gently fold in the fresh blueberries, taking care not to crush them.

4. Assemble the Cake:

- Pour the cake batter into the prepared cake tin and spread evenly with a spatula.
- Sprinkle the almond streusel topping evenly over the cake batter.

5. Bake the Cake:

- Bake in the preheated oven for 40-45 minutes, or until a skewer inserted into the center comes out clean and the top is golden brown.
- Remove from the oven and let the cake cool in the tin for 10 minutes.
- Transfer the cake to a wire rack to cool completely.

6. Decorate and Serve:

- Once cooled, dust the top of the cake with icing sugar (powdered sugar), if desired.
- Garnish with fresh blueberries before serving, if desired.

7. Serve and Enjoy:

- Slice and serve the blueberry and almond cake at room temperature.
- Enjoy the moist and nutty flavor of almonds combined with bursts of sweetness from the fresh blueberries!

Notes:

- **Storage:** Store any leftover cake in an airtight container at room temperature for up to 3-4 days.
- **Variation:** You can substitute fresh blueberries with other berries like raspberries or blackberries, depending on your preference and availability.

This blueberry and almond cake is perfect for afternoon tea, brunch, or as a dessert for any occasion. It's simple to make yet impressive in flavor, making it a favorite among those who love the combination of almonds and berries!

Mango and coconut cake

Ingredients:

For the Cake:

- 200g unsalted butter, softened
- 200g caster sugar (superfine sugar)
- 4 large eggs
- 1 teaspoon vanilla extract
- 200g self-raising flour
- 100g desiccated coconut
- 100ml coconut milk
- 1 ripe mango, peeled and diced (about 200g)

For the Mango Cream Cheese Frosting:

- 150g cream cheese, softened
- 50g unsalted butter, softened
- 300g icing sugar (powdered sugar), sifted
- 1 ripe mango, pureed (about 150g puree)

For Decoration (optional):

- Toasted coconut flakes
- Fresh mango slices
- Edible flowers

Instructions:

1. Preheat the Oven and Prepare the Pan:

- Preheat your oven to 180°C (350°F). Grease and line two 8-inch (20cm) round cake pans with parchment paper.

2. Make the Cake:

- In a large mixing bowl, cream together the softened butter and caster sugar until light and fluffy.
- Add the eggs, one at a time, beating well after each addition. Mix in the vanilla extract.
- Fold in the self-raising flour and desiccated coconut until just combined.
- Gradually add the coconut milk, stirring until the batter is smooth and well combined.
- Gently fold in the diced mango.

3. Bake the Cake:

- Divide the batter evenly between the prepared cake pans and smooth the tops with a spatula.
- Bake in the preheated oven for 25-30 minutes, or until a skewer inserted into the center of the cakes comes out clean.
- Remove from the oven and let the cakes cool in the pans for 10 minutes.
- Transfer the cakes to a wire rack to cool completely.

4. Make the Mango Cream Cheese Frosting:

- In a mixing bowl, beat together the softened cream cheese and butter until smooth and creamy.
- Gradually add the sifted icing sugar, one cup at a time, beating well after each addition.
- Mix in the pureed mango until the frosting is smooth and well combined. Adjust consistency with more icing sugar if needed.

5. Assemble the Cake:

- Place one cooled cake layer on a serving plate or cake stand.
- Spread a layer of mango cream cheese frosting over the top of the cake layer.
- Place the second cake layer on top and press gently to sandwich the layers together.
- Frost the top and sides of the cake with the remaining mango cream cheese frosting, using a spatula to create smooth or textured swirls.

6. Decorate the Cake:

- Sprinkle toasted coconut flakes over the top of the cake for added texture and flavor.
- Garnish with fresh mango slices and edible flowers, if desired, for a beautiful presentation.

7. Chill and Serve:

- Chill the Mango and Coconut Cake in the refrigerator for at least 1 hour before serving to allow the flavors to meld and the frosting to set.
- Slice and serve the cake chilled or at room temperature, and enjoy the tropical flavors of mango and coconut!

Notes:

- **Storage:** Store any leftover cake in an airtight container in the refrigerator for up to 3-4 days.
- **Fresh Mango:** Use ripe mangoes for the best flavor and sweetness in both the cake and the frosting.
- **Variation:** For a lighter frosting, you can substitute whipped cream stabilized with a bit of powdered sugar and vanilla instead of cream cheese frosting.

This Mango and Coconut Cake is perfect for summer gatherings, celebrations, or whenever you crave a taste of the tropics. It's moist, flavorful, and sure to impress with its delicious combination of mango and coconut!

Pineapple upside-down cake

Ingredients:

For the Pineapple Topping:

- 1/4 cup (60g) unsalted butter
- 1/2 cup (100g) light brown sugar, packed
- 1 can (20 oz) pineapple slices in juice (about 8 slices)
- Maraschino cherries, drained and patted dry (optional)

For the Cake Batter:

- 1 1/2 cups (190g) all-purpose flour
- 1 1/2 teaspoons baking powder
- 1/4 teaspoon salt
- 1/2 cup (115g) unsalted butter, softened
- 1 cup (200g) granulated sugar
- 2 large eggs
- 1 teaspoon vanilla extract
- 1/2 cup (120ml) pineapple juice (reserved from the canned pineapple)
- 1/4 cup (60ml) milk

Instructions:

1. Prepare the Pineapple Topping:

- Preheat your oven to 350°F (175°C). Grease a 9-inch round cake pan (preferably with high sides) and line the bottom with parchment paper.
- Melt the unsalted butter in a small saucepan over medium heat. Once melted, add the brown sugar and stir until dissolved and bubbly. Pour this mixture into the prepared cake pan, spreading it evenly across the bottom.
- Arrange the pineapple slices over the caramelized sugar mixture in a single layer. Place maraschino cherries in the center of each pineapple slice, if using.

2. Make the Cake Batter:

- In a medium bowl, whisk together the all-purpose flour, baking powder, and salt. Set aside.
- In a large mixing bowl, cream together the softened unsalted butter and granulated sugar until light and fluffy.
- Add the eggs, one at a time, beating well after each addition. Mix in the vanilla extract.
- Gradually add the dry flour mixture to the butter mixture, alternating with additions of pineapple juice and milk, beginning and ending with the flour mixture. Mix until just combined, being careful not to overmix.

3. Assemble and Bake the Cake:

- Carefully spoon the cake batter over the pineapple slices in the cake pan, spreading it evenly with a spatula.
- Tap the cake pan gently on the counter to release any air bubbles.
- Bake in the preheated oven for 35-40 minutes, or until a toothpick inserted into the center of the cake comes out clean.

4. Cool and Invert the Cake:

- Remove the cake from the oven and let it cool in the pan for about 10 minutes.
- Place a serving plate upside down over the cake pan, then carefully invert the cake onto the plate. Slowly lift off the cake pan, being cautious of any hot caramelized sugar that may drip.
- If any pineapple slices or cherries stick to the pan, gently remove them and place them back onto the cake.

5. Serve and Enjoy:

- Allow the cake to cool slightly before slicing and serving. Serve warm or at room temperature.

Notes:

- **Pineapple Juice:** Using reserved pineapple juice adds extra flavor to the cake batter.
- **Storage:** Store any leftover cake covered at room temperature for up to 3-4 days. Warm slices briefly in the microwave before serving if desired.

This pineapple upside-down cake is a nostalgic and comforting dessert that's perfect for any occasion. The combination of caramelized pineapple, sweet cherries, and buttery cake is sure to be a hit with family and friends!

Vanilla slice

Ingredients:

For the pastry layers:

- 2 sheets of ready-rolled puff pastry (about 9x9 inches each)
- 1 egg, beaten (for egg wash)
- Powdered sugar, for dusting (optional)

For the vanilla custard filling:

- 2 cups whole milk
- 1/2 cup granulated sugar
- 4 egg yolks
- 1/4 cup cornstarch
- 1 teaspoon vanilla extract
- Pinch of salt

Instructions:

1. **Prepare the Pastry Layers:**
    - Preheat your oven to 400°F (200°C).
    - Place one sheet of puff pastry on a baking sheet lined with parchment paper.
    - Prick the pastry with a fork to prevent it from puffing up too much during baking.
    - Brush the pastry with beaten egg wash.
    - Bake in the preheated oven for about 15-20 minutes, or until golden brown and puffed up.
    - Remove from the oven and let it cool completely on a wire rack.
2. **Bake the Second Pastry Layer:**
    - Repeat the same process with the second sheet of puff pastry. Prick, brush with egg wash, and bake until golden brown. Let it cool completely.
3. **Prepare the Vanilla Custard Filling:**
    - In a saucepan, heat the milk over medium heat until it just begins to simmer. Remove from heat.
    - In a mixing bowl, whisk together sugar, egg yolks, cornstarch, vanilla extract, and salt until smooth and creamy.
    - Gradually pour the hot milk into the egg mixture, whisking constantly to prevent curdling.
    - Return the mixture to the saucepan and cook over medium heat, stirring constantly, until the custard thickens and coats the back of a spoon (about 5-7 minutes).
    - Remove from heat and transfer the custard to a bowl. Place a piece of plastic wrap directly on the surface of the custard to prevent a skin from forming. Let it cool to room temperature.

4. **Assemble the Vanilla Slice:**
    - Place one sheet of baked puff pastry on a serving platter.
    - Spread the cooled vanilla custard evenly over the pastry layer.
    - Carefully place the second pastry layer on top of the custard.
    - Lightly dust the top with powdered sugar, if desired.
5. **Chill and Serve:**
    - Refrigerate the assembled vanilla slice for at least 1-2 hours to allow the custard to set.
    - Once chilled and set, use a sharp knife to cut into squares or rectangles.
    - Serve cold and enjoy!

Tips:

- Ensure the custard is completely cooled before assembling the vanilla slice to prevent the pastry from becoming soggy.
- You can also add a layer of whipped cream or a thin layer of icing on top of the custard before placing the second pastry layer for variation.
- Store any leftover vanilla slice in the refrigerator, covered, for up to 2-3 days.

This recipe yields a delicious vanilla slice with crisp layers of puff pastry and creamy vanilla custard—a perfect treat for any occasion!

Passionfruit tart

Ingredients:

For the pastry crust:

- 1 1/4 cups all-purpose flour
- 1/4 cup granulated sugar
- 1/4 teaspoon salt
- 1/2 cup unsalted butter, cold and cut into small cubes
- 1 egg yolk
- 1-2 tablespoons cold water

For the passionfruit curd:

- 1/2 cup passionfruit pulp (about 5-6 passionfruits)
- 1/2 cup granulated sugar
- 3 egg yolks
- 1/4 cup unsalted butter, cut into small cubes
- Zest of 1 lemon (optional, for added flavor)

For garnish (optional):

- Fresh berries (such as raspberries or strawberries)
- Mint leaves
- Powdered sugar for dusting

Instructions:

1. **Make the pastry crust:**
    - In a food processor, combine flour, sugar, and salt. Pulse a few times to mix.
    - Add cold cubed butter and pulse until the mixture resembles coarse crumbs.
    - Add egg yolk and 1 tablespoon of cold water. Pulse until the dough starts to come together. Add more water, if needed, but do not overmix.
    - Turn the dough out onto a lightly floured surface and gently knead it a few times to bring it together into a ball.
    - Flatten the dough into a disk, wrap it in plastic wrap, and refrigerate for at least 30 minutes.
2. **Preheat the oven:**
    - Preheat your oven to 375°F (190°C).
3. **Roll out the pastry:**
    - On a lightly floured surface, roll out the chilled pastry dough into a circle large enough to line a 9-inch tart pan.
    - Carefully transfer the rolled-out dough to the tart pan, pressing it gently into the bottom and sides. Trim any excess dough hanging over the edges.

4. **Blind bake the crust:**
   - Line the pastry with parchment paper or aluminum foil and fill with pie weights, dried beans, or rice.
   - Bake in the preheated oven for about 15 minutes.
   - Remove the parchment paper and weights, then bake for another 10-12 minutes, or until the crust is golden brown. Remove from the oven and let it cool completely on a wire rack.
5. **Make the passionfruit curd:**
   - In a saucepan, combine passionfruit pulp, sugar, and lemon zest (if using). Heat over medium heat until the mixture just begins to simmer, stirring occasionally.
   - In a separate bowl, whisk the egg yolks until smooth.
   - Gradually pour the hot passionfruit mixture into the egg yolks, whisking constantly to temper the eggs.
   - Return the mixture to the saucepan and cook over medium-low heat, stirring constantly with a wooden spoon or spatula, until it thickens enough to coat the back of the spoon (about 5-7 minutes).
   - Remove from heat and stir in the cubed butter until melted and well combined.
   - Strain the curd through a fine mesh sieve into a clean bowl to remove any solids. Let it cool slightly.
6. **Assemble the tart:**
   - Pour the warm passionfruit curd into the cooled tart shell, spreading it evenly with a spatula.
   - Refrigerate the tart for at least 1-2 hours to allow the curd to set.
7. **Garnish and serve:**
   - Before serving, garnish the tart with fresh berries, mint leaves, and a dusting of powdered sugar, if desired.
   - Slice and serve chilled. Enjoy your delicious passionfruit tart!

Tips:

- Choose ripe and fragrant passionfruits for the best flavor in your curd.
- Make sure the tart shell is completely cooled before adding the curd to prevent it from becoming soggy.
- You can store any leftover tart in the refrigerator, covered, for up to 2-3 days.

This passionfruit tart recipe delivers a balance of sweet and tart flavors with a buttery crust that melts in your mouth—a perfect dessert for summer or any special occasion!

Caramel slice

Ingredients:

For the shortbread base:

- 1 cup all-purpose flour
- 1/3 cup granulated sugar
- 1/2 cup unsalted butter, softened

For the caramel filling:

- 1/2 cup unsalted butter
- 1/2 cup packed light brown sugar
- 1 (14 oz) can sweetened condensed milk

For the chocolate topping:

- 6 oz (170g) semi-sweet or dark chocolate, chopped
- 1 tablespoon unsalted butter

Instructions:

1. **Make the shortbread base:**
    - Preheat your oven to 350°F (175°C). Grease and line a 9-inch square baking pan with parchment paper, leaving an overhang for easy removal later.
    - In a mixing bowl, combine the flour, sugar, and softened butter. Mix until the mixture resembles fine breadcrumbs and starts to come together.
    - Press the mixture evenly into the prepared baking pan using your fingers or the back of a spoon.
    - Bake in the preheated oven for 15-20 minutes, or until the shortbread base is lightly golden. Remove from the oven and let it cool in the pan while you prepare the caramel filling.
2. **Make the caramel filling:**
    - In a medium saucepan, melt the butter over medium heat.
    - Add the brown sugar and sweetened condensed milk, stirring continuously.
    - Bring the mixture to a gentle boil, then reduce the heat to low. Simmer for about 5-7 minutes, stirring constantly, until the mixture thickens and turns a golden caramel color.
    - Remove from heat and immediately pour the hot caramel evenly over the cooled shortbread base. Use a spatula to spread it out if needed.
    - Allow the caramel layer to cool completely and set in the pan.
3. **Make the chocolate topping:**
    - In a microwave-safe bowl or using a double boiler, melt the chopped chocolate and tablespoon of butter together until smooth and glossy.

- Pour the melted chocolate over the cooled caramel layer, spreading it out evenly with a spatula.
4. **Chill and serve:**
    - Refrigerate the caramel slice for at least 1-2 hours, or until the chocolate topping has set.
    - Once set, lift the slice out of the pan using the parchment paper overhang. Transfer to a cutting board and cut into squares or rectangles.
    - Serve chilled and enjoy!

Tips:

- Make sure each layer is cooled and set before adding the next layer to prevent them from mixing.
- You can sprinkle a pinch of sea salt over the caramel layer before adding the chocolate topping for a delicious salty-sweet contrast.
- Store any leftover caramel slice in an airtight container in the refrigerator for up to 5 days.

This caramel slice recipe yields a wonderfully rich and indulgent dessert with its buttery shortbread, chewy caramel, and smooth chocolate layers—a perfect treat for any occasion!

Coffee cake

Ingredients:

For the cake batter:

- 1/2 cup unsalted butter, softened
- 1 cup granulated sugar
- 2 eggs
- 1 teaspoon vanilla extract
- 1 cup sour cream or plain Greek yogurt
- 2 cups all-purpose flour
- 1 teaspoon baking powder
- 1 teaspoon baking soda
- 1/2 teaspoon salt

For the streusel topping:

- 1/2 cup packed brown sugar
- 1/2 cup all-purpose flour
- 1 teaspoon ground cinnamon
- 1/4 cup cold unsalted butter, cut into small cubes
- 1/2 cup chopped nuts (optional, such as walnuts or pecans)

For the optional glaze:

- 1/2 cup powdered sugar
- 1-2 tablespoons milk or cream
- 1/2 teaspoon vanilla extract

Instructions:

1. **Preheat your oven and prepare the pan:**
   - Preheat your oven to 350°F (175°C). Grease and flour a 9x13-inch baking pan, or line it with parchment paper for easy removal.
2. **Make the streusel topping:**
   - In a small bowl, combine the brown sugar, flour, cinnamon, and cold butter cubes.
   - Using a pastry cutter or your fingers, blend the mixture until it resembles coarse crumbs. Stir in the chopped nuts if using. Set aside.
3. **Make the cake batter:**
   - In a large mixing bowl, cream together the softened butter and granulated sugar until light and fluffy.
   - Add the eggs, one at a time, beating well after each addition. Stir in the vanilla extract.

- Add the sour cream or Greek yogurt and mix until smooth and well combined.
- In a separate bowl, whisk together the flour, baking powder, baking soda, and salt.
- Gradually add the dry ingredients to the wet ingredients, mixing until just combined. Do not overmix.

4. **Assemble and bake:**
    - Spread half of the batter evenly into the prepared baking pan.
    - Sprinkle half of the streusel topping over the batter.
    - Carefully spread the remaining batter over the streusel layer.
    - Sprinkle the remaining streusel topping evenly over the top of the cake batter.

5. **Bake the coffee cake:**
    - Bake in the preheated oven for 30-35 minutes, or until a toothpick inserted into the center comes out clean and the top is golden brown.
    - Remove from the oven and let the coffee cake cool in the pan on a wire rack.

6. **Optional glaze:**
    - If desired, whisk together the powdered sugar, milk or cream, and vanilla extract until smooth.
    - Drizzle the glaze over the cooled coffee cake before serving.

7. **Serve and enjoy:**
    - Slice the coffee cake into squares or rectangles.
    - Serve warm or at room temperature with your favorite hot beverage.

Tips:

- Ensure your butter and eggs are at room temperature for smooth incorporation into the batter.
- Feel free to customize the streusel topping by adding oats or adjusting the amount of cinnamon to your preference.
- Store any leftover coffee cake in an airtight container at room temperature for up to 3 days, or refrigerate for longer freshness.

This coffee cake recipe is perfect for breakfast, brunch, or as a comforting dessert. Its moist texture, cinnamon-scented streusel topping, and optional glaze make it a delightful treat to enjoy any time of day!

Neenish tart

Ingredients:

For the pastry:

- 1 1/2 cups all-purpose flour
- 1/2 cup unsalted butter, cold and cut into cubes
- 1/4 cup granulated sugar
- 1 egg yolk
- 2-3 tablespoons cold water

For the filling:

- 1/2 cup raspberry jam (or other fruit jam of your choice)

For the icing:

- 1 cup powdered sugar (icing sugar)
- 1 tablespoon cocoa powder (for chocolate icing)
- 1 tablespoon lemon juice (for lemon icing)
- 1-2 tablespoons boiling water, as needed

Instructions:

1. **Make the pastry:**
   - In a food processor, pulse together the flour and cold butter cubes until the mixture resembles breadcrumbs.
   - Add the sugar and pulse again briefly to combine.
   - Add the egg yolk and 2 tablespoons of cold water. Pulse until the mixture starts to come together. If needed, add an additional tablespoon of water, a little at a time, until the dough forms a ball.
   - Wrap the dough in plastic wrap and refrigerate for at least 30 minutes.
2. **Prepare the tart shells:**
   - Preheat your oven to 375°F (190°C). Lightly grease a 12-hole tart pan or muffin tin.
   - On a lightly floured surface, roll out the chilled pastry dough to about 1/8 inch thickness.
   - Use a round cookie cutter or glass slightly larger than the tart molds to cut out circles of pastry.
   - Press each pastry circle into the tart molds, gently pressing the dough into the bottom and sides. Trim any excess dough.
   - Prick the bases of the pastry with a fork to prevent them from puffing up during baking.
   - Bake in the preheated oven for 12-15 minutes, or until lightly golden brown.

- Remove from the oven and allow the tart shells to cool completely in the pan.
3. **Fill the tart shells:**
    - Once the tart shells are cooled, spoon about 1 teaspoon of raspberry jam (or your chosen fruit jam) into each tart shell. Spread it out evenly with the back of a spoon.
4. **Make the icing:**
    - In two separate bowls, prepare the icing. For the vanilla icing, sift the powdered sugar into a bowl and stir in enough boiling water to make a smooth, spreadable consistency. Add lemon juice for flavor if desired.
    - For the chocolate icing, sift the powdered sugar and cocoa powder into another bowl. Add enough boiling water to make a smooth, spreadable consistency.
5. **Ice the tarts:**
    - Spread half of each tart with vanilla or lemon icing and the other half with chocolate icing, creating a two-tone effect.
    - Allow the icing to set before serving.
6. **Serve and enjoy:**
    - Neenish tarts are best served at room temperature. Enjoy them as a delightful treat with tea or coffee!

Tips:

- You can customize the flavors of the icing to suit your preferences. Some variations include using orange juice and zest for the icing, or even adding a bit of peppermint extract for a refreshing twist.
- Store Neenish tarts in an airtight container at room temperature for up to 3 days.

These Neenish tarts are sure to be a hit with their buttery pastry, fruity jam filling, and contrasting vanilla/lemon and chocolate icing layers—a perfect treat for any occasion!

Scones

Ingredients:

- 2 cups all-purpose flour
- 1/4 cup granulated sugar
- 1 tablespoon baking powder
- 1/2 teaspoon salt
- 1/3 cup unsalted butter, cold and cut into small cubes
- 1/2 cup milk (plus extra for brushing)
- 1 large egg
- 1 teaspoon vanilla extract (optional)

Instructions:

1. **Preheat your oven:**
   - Preheat your oven to 400°F (200°C). Line a baking sheet with parchment paper or lightly grease it.
2. **Mix dry ingredients:**
   - In a large mixing bowl, whisk together the flour, sugar, baking powder, and salt.
3. **Cut in the butter:**
   - Add the cold butter cubes to the flour mixture. Using a pastry cutter or your fingertips, rub the butter into the flour until the mixture resembles coarse crumbs and there are no large butter pieces remaining.
4. **Combine wet ingredients:**
   - In a separate bowl, whisk together the milk, egg, and vanilla extract (if using).
5. **Form the dough:**
   - Make a well in the center of the dry ingredients. Pour the wet ingredients into the well.
   - Use a fork or spatula to gently mix the ingredients together until just combined. Be careful not to overmix; the dough should be slightly sticky.
6. **Shape the scones:**
   - Transfer the dough onto a lightly floured surface. Gently knead the dough a few times until it comes together.
   - Pat the dough into a circle or rectangle, about 3/4 to 1 inch thick.
7. **Cut out the scones:**
   - Use a floured round cutter (about 2.5 inches in diameter) to cut out scones from the dough. Press straight down without twisting the cutter to ensure the scones rise evenly.
   - Place the scones on the prepared baking sheet, spacing them about 2 inches apart.
8. **Bake the scones:**
   - Brush the tops of the scones lightly with milk to help them brown.

- Bake in the preheated oven for 12-15 minutes, or until the scones are golden brown on top and cooked through. They should sound hollow when tapped on the bottom.
9. **Serve and enjoy:**
    - Remove the scones from the oven and transfer them to a wire rack to cool slightly.
    - Serve warm with clotted cream, jam, and a cup of tea or coffee.

Tips:

- For variations, you can add dried fruits such as raisins or currants to the dry ingredients before adding the wet ingredients.
- Handle the dough as little as possible to ensure light and fluffy scones.
- If you prefer a more traditional approach, you can use buttermilk instead of regular milk for a tangier flavor.

These homemade scones are perfect for a cozy breakfast or an elegant afternoon tea. Their buttery, crumbly texture and delightful flavor make them a beloved treat enjoyed by many around the world.

Fairy bread

Ingredients:

- Slices of white bread (you can use any type of soft white bread)
- Butter or margarine, softened
- Hundreds and thousands (sprinkles/nonpareils)

Instructions:

1. **Prepare the bread:**
   - Lay out slices of white bread on a clean surface.
2. **Spread with butter:**
   - Spread a generous layer of softened butter or margarine evenly over each slice of bread. Make sure to cover the entire surface to the edges.
3. **Add sprinkles:**
   - Sprinkle hundreds and thousands (or your choice of colorful sprinkles) liberally over the buttered bread slices. Ensure the sprinkles cover the buttered surface evenly.
4. **Cut and serve:**
   - Using a sharp knife, cut each slice of fairy bread into triangles, squares, or rectangles, depending on your preference and the occasion.
5. **Serve and enjoy:**
   - Arrange the fairy bread on a serving platter or plate and serve immediately. It's best enjoyed fresh and at room temperature.

Tips:

- Use fresh, soft bread for the best texture.
- You can customize fairy bread by using different types of sprinkles or adding a thin layer of cream cheese under the butter for extra richness.
- Fairy bread is a fun and easy treat that's perfect for kids' parties or any celebration where you want to add a touch of colorful whimsy.

This simple yet delightful treat captures the joy and innocence of childhood parties and is sure to bring smiles to both kids and adults alike!

Honeycomb cake

Ingredients:

- 1 cup granulated sugar
- 1/4 cup golden syrup or light corn syrup
- 1 tablespoon water
- 1 tablespoon baking soda
- Optional: 6 oz (170g) dark or milk chocolate, melted (for dipping or drizzling)

Instructions:

1. **Prepare a baking sheet:**
    - Line a baking sheet with parchment paper or grease it lightly with butter. Set aside.
2. **Combine sugar, syrup, and water:**
    - In a medium-sized heavy-bottomed saucepan, combine the sugar, golden syrup (or corn syrup), and water over medium heat. Stir until the sugar dissolves.
3. **Cook the mixture:**
    - Once the sugar has dissolved, stop stirring and allow the mixture to come to a boil. Insert a candy thermometer into the mixture and cook until it reaches 300°F (150°C), also known as the hard crack stage.
4. **Add baking soda:**
    - Remove the saucepan from the heat. Quickly add the baking soda to the sugar mixture and stir gently but quickly. The mixture will foam up and increase in volume.
5. **Pour onto the baking sheet:**
    - Immediately pour the foaming mixture onto the prepared baking sheet. Spread it out quickly with a spatula or the back of a spoon, but avoid pressing down too much as it will deflate the honeycomb structure.
6. **Let it cool and set:**
    - Allow the honeycomb cake to cool and set completely at room temperature for about 1 hour. It will harden as it cools.
7. **Break into pieces:**
    - Once fully cooled and hardened, break the honeycomb cake into pieces of your desired size using your hands or a knife.
8. **Optional: Dip or drizzle with chocolate:**
    - If desired, melt the chocolate in a heatproof bowl over a pot of simmering water (double boiler method). Dip the honeycomb pieces into the melted chocolate or drizzle the chocolate over them. Place them on a parchment-lined baking sheet to set.
9. **Store and enjoy:**
    - Store the honeycomb cake in an airtight container at room temperature. It's best enjoyed within a few days for optimal crunchiness.

Tips:

- Be careful when handling hot sugar syrup as it can cause severe burns.
- Work quickly once you add the baking soda as the mixture will set fast.
- Customize your honeycomb cake by adding chopped nuts, sea salt, or spices like cinnamon to the mixture before pouring onto the baking sheet.

This honeycomb cake recipe yields a delightful crunchy treat that's perfect for snacking, garnishing desserts, or giving as homemade gifts. Enjoy the sweet, airy texture and the satisfying crackle of each bite!

Raspberry friand

Ingredients:

- 1 cup almond meal (ground almonds)
- 1 cup powdered sugar (icing sugar), sifted
- 1/2 cup all-purpose flour
- 1/2 teaspoon baking powder
- Pinch of salt
- Zest of 1 lemon (optional, for added flavor)
- 5 egg whites
- 1/2 cup unsalted butter, melted and cooled
- 1/2 teaspoon vanilla extract
- 1 cup fresh raspberries (or frozen raspberries, thawed and drained)

Instructions:

1. **Preheat your oven:**
   - Preheat the oven to 350°F (175°C). Grease a 12-cup muffin tin or friand pan well with butter or cooking spray.
2. **Prepare dry ingredients:**
   - In a mixing bowl, combine the almond meal, powdered sugar, flour, baking powder, salt, and lemon zest (if using). Stir until well combined.
3. **Whisk egg whites:**
   - In a separate bowl, whisk the egg whites until frothy but not stiff.
4. **Combine wet ingredients:**
   - Make a well in the center of the dry ingredients. Pour in the melted butter and vanilla extract. Add the frothy egg whites. Gently fold the mixture together until just combined. Be careful not to overmix; the batter should be smooth and thick.
5. **Add raspberries:**
   - Gently fold in the raspberries, being careful not to break them up too much.
6. **Fill the muffin tin:**
   - Spoon the batter evenly into the prepared muffin tin or friand pan, filling each cup about 2/3 full.
7. **Bake the friands:**
   - Bake in the preheated oven for 20-25 minutes, or until the tops are golden brown and a toothpick inserted into the center comes out clean.
8. **Cool and serve:**
   - Allow the raspberry friands to cool in the pan for 5 minutes, then transfer them to a wire rack to cool completely.
9. **Optional: Dust with powdered sugar:**
   - Once cooled, dust the tops of the raspberry friands with powdered sugar for a decorative touch.
10. **Serve and enjoy:**

- Serve the raspberry friands warm or at room temperature. They are delicious on their own or with a dollop of whipped cream or a scoop of vanilla ice cream.

Tips:

- If you don't have almond meal, you can make your own by pulsing blanched almonds in a food processor until finely ground.
- Ensure your melted butter is cooled before adding it to the batter to prevent cooking the egg whites.
- You can substitute raspberries with other berries like blueberries or strawberries if preferred.

These raspberry friands are perfect for morning or afternoon tea, or as a sweet treat any time of day. Their moist, almond-rich texture and bursts of raspberry flavor make them a delightful addition to any dessert table.

White chocolate and macadamia cake

Ingredients:

For the cake:

- 1 cup unsalted butter, softened
- 1 cup granulated sugar
- 4 large eggs
- 1 teaspoon vanilla extract
- 2 cups all-purpose flour
- 2 teaspoons baking powder
- 1/2 teaspoon salt
- 1/2 cup milk
- 1 cup white chocolate chips or chopped white chocolate
- 1 cup macadamia nuts, roughly chopped

For the frosting:

- 1/2 cup unsalted butter, softened
- 8 oz (225g) white chocolate, melted and cooled
- 2 cups powdered sugar (icing sugar)
- 1 teaspoon vanilla extract
- 2-4 tablespoons milk or cream, as needed

Optional garnish:

- Additional chopped macadamia nuts
- White chocolate curls or shavings

Instructions:

1. **Preheat your oven:**
   - Preheat the oven to 350°F (175°C). Grease and flour two 9-inch round cake pans, or line them with parchment paper for easy removal.
2. **Prepare the cake batter:**
   - In a large mixing bowl, cream together the softened butter and granulated sugar until light and fluffy.
   - Add the eggs one at a time, beating well after each addition. Stir in the vanilla extract.
3. **Combine dry ingredients:**
   - In a separate bowl, whisk together the flour, baking powder, and salt.
4. **Alternate additions:**
   - Gradually add the dry ingredients to the creamed mixture, alternating with the milk. Begin and end with the dry ingredients.

- Fold in the white chocolate chips or chopped white chocolate and the chopped macadamia nuts.
5. **Bake the cakes:**
    - Divide the batter evenly between the prepared cake pans.
    - Bake in the preheated oven for 25-30 minutes, or until a toothpick inserted into the center comes out clean.
    - Remove from the oven and allow the cakes to cool in the pans for 10 minutes before transferring them to wire racks to cool completely.
6. **Make the frosting:**
    - In a mixing bowl, beat the softened butter until creamy. Gradually add the melted and cooled white chocolate, mixing until well combined.
    - Add the powdered sugar and vanilla extract, beating until smooth and creamy. Adjust the consistency with milk or cream as needed to achieve a spreadable frosting.
7. **Assemble the cake:**
    - Place one cake layer on a serving plate or cake stand. Spread a generous layer of frosting over the top.
    - Carefully place the second cake layer on top. Spread the remaining frosting evenly over the top and sides of the cake.
8. **Optional garnish:**
    - Sprinkle additional chopped macadamia nuts over the top of the cake.
    - Garnish with white chocolate curls or shavings for an elegant finish.
9. **Chill and serve:**
    - For best results, chill the cake in the refrigerator for about 30 minutes before serving to set the frosting.
    - Slice and serve the white chocolate and macadamia cake. Enjoy the luxurious combination of flavors and textures!

Tips:

- Make sure the melted white chocolate for the frosting is cooled to room temperature before adding it to the butter.
- You can adjust the sweetness of the frosting by adding more or less powdered sugar according to your taste.
- Store any leftover cake covered in the refrigerator. Bring it to room temperature before serving for the best texture and flavor.

This white chocolate and macadamia cake is sure to impress with its rich flavors and moist texture. It's perfect for special occasions or as a delightful treat for white chocolate and nut lovers!

Marmalade cake

Ingredients:

- 1 cup unsalted butter, softened
- 1 cup granulated sugar
- 4 large eggs
- 2 cups all-purpose flour
- 1 teaspoon baking powder
- 1/2 teaspoon baking soda
- 1/4 teaspoon salt
- 1 cup orange marmalade
- Zest of 1 orange (optional, for extra flavor)
- 1/4 cup freshly squeezed orange juice
- 1/2 cup plain yogurt or sour cream
- Powdered sugar, for dusting (optional)

Instructions:

1. **Preheat your oven:**
   - Preheat the oven to 350°F (175°C). Grease and flour a 9-inch round cake pan or line it with parchment paper.
2. **Cream the butter and sugar:**
   - In a large mixing bowl, cream together the softened butter and granulated sugar until light and fluffy.
3. **Add eggs:**
   - Add the eggs one at a time, beating well after each addition.
4. **Combine dry ingredients:**
   - In a separate bowl, whisk together the flour, baking powder, baking soda, and salt.
5. **Mix wet ingredients:**
   - In another bowl, combine the orange marmalade, orange zest (if using), orange juice, and plain yogurt or sour cream. Mix until well combined.
6. **Combine and mix:**
   - Gradually add the dry ingredients to the creamed butter and sugar mixture, alternating with the wet ingredients mixture. Begin and end with the dry ingredients.
   - Mix until just combined. Do not overmix.
7. **Bake the cake:**
   - Pour the batter into the prepared cake pan and smooth the top with a spatula.
   - Bake in the preheated oven for 40-45 minutes, or until a toothpick inserted into the center comes out clean.
8. **Cool and serve:**

- Allow the cake to cool in the pan for 10 minutes, then transfer it to a wire rack to cool completely.

9. **Dust with powdered sugar (optional):**
   - Once cooled, dust the top of the cake with powdered sugar for a decorative finish.

10. **Slice and enjoy:**
    - Slice the marmalade cake and serve it as is, or with a dollop of whipped cream or a scoop of vanilla ice cream.

Tips:

- Use good quality orange marmalade for the best flavor.
- You can adjust the amount of marmalade to suit your taste preferences.
- Store leftover cake in an airtight container at room temperature for up to 3 days.

This marmalade cake is perfect for tea time or as a dessert for citrus lovers. It's moist, flavorful, and showcases the delightful tangy sweetness of orange marmalade in every bite!

Strawberry sponge cake

Ingredients:

For the sponge cake:

- 4 large eggs, at room temperature
- 1 cup granulated sugar
- 1 teaspoon vanilla extract
- 1 cup cake flour (or 3/4 cup all-purpose flour + 1/4 cup cornstarch)
- 1 teaspoon baking powder
- 1/4 teaspoon salt

For the strawberry filling:

- 2 cups fresh strawberries, hulled and sliced
- 1/4 cup granulated sugar
- 1 tablespoon lemon juice

For the whipped cream frosting:

- 2 cups heavy cream, chilled
- 1/4 cup powdered sugar (icing sugar)
- 1 teaspoon vanilla extract

Optional:

- Fresh strawberries, for garnish

Instructions:

1. **Prepare the sponge cake:**
    - Preheat your oven to 350°F (175°C). Grease and line two 9-inch round cake pans with parchment paper.
    - In a large mixing bowl, beat the eggs and granulated sugar together using an electric mixer on high speed until pale, fluffy, and doubled in volume. This can take about 5-7 minutes.
    - Beat in the vanilla extract.
    - In a separate bowl, sift together the cake flour, baking powder, and salt.
    - Gently fold the flour mixture into the egg mixture in three additions, using a spatula. Be careful not to deflate the batter too much.
    - Divide the batter evenly between the prepared cake pans and smooth the tops with a spatula.
    - Bake in the preheated oven for 20-25 minutes, or until the cakes are golden and spring back when lightly touched.

- Remove from the oven and let the cakes cool in the pans for 10 minutes before transferring them to a wire rack to cool completely.
2. **Prepare the strawberry filling:**
    - In a bowl, toss together the sliced strawberries, granulated sugar, and lemon juice. Let them macerate for about 15-20 minutes to release their juices.
3. **Make the whipped cream frosting:**
    - In a chilled mixing bowl, whip the heavy cream, powdered sugar, and vanilla extract together until stiff peaks form.
4. **Assemble the cake:**
    - Place one cooled sponge cake layer on a serving plate or cake stand.
    - Spread half of the whipped cream over the cake layer, then spoon half of the macerated strawberries (without too much liquid) over the whipped cream.
    - Place the second cake layer on top and gently press down.
    - Spread the remaining whipped cream over the top of the cake.
    - Arrange the remaining macerated strawberries on top of the whipped cream.
5. **Garnish (optional):**
    - Garnish the cake with fresh whole strawberries or additional sliced strawberries.
6. **Chill and serve:**
    - Chill the cake in the refrigerator for at least 1 hour before serving to allow the flavors to meld together.
7. **Slice and enjoy:**
    - Slice the strawberry sponge cake and serve chilled. Enjoy the light, fluffy texture of the sponge cake paired with the freshness of strawberries and creamy whipped cream!

Tips:

- Make sure to handle the sponge cake layers gently to prevent them from deflating.
- You can adjust the sweetness of the whipped cream frosting and strawberry filling according to your preference.
- This cake is best served the day it is assembled, as the sponge cake can absorb moisture from the strawberries and whipped cream.

This strawberry sponge cake is perfect for special occasions, birthdays, or any time you want to enjoy a light and fruity dessert. It's sure to be a hit with strawberry lovers!

Peanut butter cake

Ingredients:

For the cake:

- 1/2 cup unsalted butter, softened
- 1 cup creamy peanut butter
- 1 1/2 cups granulated sugar
- 3 large eggs
- 2 teaspoons vanilla extract
- 2 cups all-purpose flour
- 2 teaspoons baking powder
- 1/2 teaspoon salt
- 1 cup milk

For the peanut butter frosting:

- 1 cup creamy peanut butter
- 1/2 cup unsalted butter, softened
- 2 cups powdered sugar (icing sugar)
- 1 teaspoon vanilla extract
- 1/4 cup heavy cream (or milk)

Optional garnish:

- Chopped peanuts
- Mini chocolate chips

Instructions:

1. **Preheat your oven:**
   - Preheat the oven to 350°F (175°C). Grease and flour two 9-inch round cake pans, or line them with parchment paper for easy removal.
2. **Make the cake batter:**
   - In a large mixing bowl, cream together the softened butter, creamy peanut butter, and granulated sugar until light and fluffy.
   - Add the eggs one at a time, beating well after each addition. Stir in the vanilla extract.
   - In a separate bowl, whisk together the flour, baking powder, and salt.
   - Gradually add the dry ingredients to the creamed mixture, alternating with the milk. Begin and end with the dry ingredients, mixing until just combined. Do not overmix.
3. **Bake the cake:**

- Divide the batter evenly between the prepared cake pans. Smooth the tops with a spatula.
- Bake in the preheated oven for 25-30 minutes, or until a toothpick inserted into the center comes out clean.
- Remove from the oven and let the cakes cool in the pans for 10 minutes before transferring them to a wire rack to cool completely.

4. **Make the peanut butter frosting:**
   - In a mixing bowl, beat together the creamy peanut butter and softened butter until smooth.
   - Gradually add the powdered sugar, one cup at a time, mixing well after each addition.
   - Add the vanilla extract and heavy cream (or milk), and beat until the frosting is smooth and creamy. Adjust the consistency with more cream or powdered sugar as needed.

5. **Assemble the cake:**
   - Place one cooled cake layer on a serving plate or cake stand.
   - Spread a generous layer of peanut butter frosting over the top of the cake layer.
   - Carefully place the second cake layer on top. Spread the remaining frosting evenly over the top and sides of the cake.

6. **Optional garnish:**
   - Garnish the cake with chopped peanuts or mini chocolate chips, if desired.

7. **Chill and serve:**
   - Chill the cake in the refrigerator for about 30 minutes before slicing and serving. This helps set the frosting and makes it easier to slice.

8. **Slice and enjoy:**
   - Slice the peanut butter cake and serve it as a delicious dessert or treat. Enjoy the rich, nutty flavor and moist texture of this peanut butter delight!

Tips:

- Make sure the butter and cream cheese are at room temperature for smooth blending.
- If you prefer a less sweet frosting, you can reduce the amount of powdered sugar to suit your taste.
- Store any leftover cake covered in the refrigerator. Bring it to room temperature before serving for the best texture and flavor.

This peanut butter cake is perfect for peanut butter lovers and makes a wonderful dessert for birthdays, parties, or any special occasion. It's sure to be a hit with its irresistible peanut butter flavor and creamy frosting!

Banana cake

Ingredients:

For the cake:

- 2 cups mashed ripe bananas (about 4-5 medium bananas)
- 1 teaspoon lemon juice (to prevent bananas from browning)
- 1 teaspoon baking soda
- 1/2 cup unsalted butter, softened
- 1 cup granulated sugar
- 2 large eggs
- 1 teaspoon vanilla extract
- 1/4 teaspoon salt
- 1 1/2 cups all-purpose flour

For the cream cheese frosting (optional):

- 8 oz (225g) cream cheese, softened
- 1/2 cup unsalted butter, softened
- 4 cups powdered sugar (icing sugar)
- 1 teaspoon vanilla extract

Instructions:

1. **Preheat your oven:**
    - Preheat the oven to 350°F (175°C). Grease and flour a 9x13-inch baking pan, or line it with parchment paper for easy removal.
2. **Prepare the mashed bananas:**
    - In a small bowl, mash the ripe bananas together with the lemon juice and baking soda. Set aside.
3. **Make the cake batter:**
    - In a large mixing bowl, cream together the softened butter and granulated sugar until light and fluffy.
    - Add the eggs one at a time, beating well after each addition. Stir in the vanilla extract and salt.
    - Gradually add the flour to the creamed mixture, mixing until just combined.
    - Fold in the mashed banana mixture until evenly incorporated.
4. **Bake the cake:**
    - Pour the batter into the prepared baking pan, spreading it out evenly with a spatula.
    - Bake in the preheated oven for 25-30 minutes, or until a toothpick inserted into the center comes out clean.
    - Remove from the oven and let the cake cool in the pan for 10 minutes before transferring it to a wire rack to cool completely.

5. **Make the cream cheese frosting (optional):**
    - In a mixing bowl, beat together the softened cream cheese and butter until smooth and creamy.
    - Gradually add the powdered sugar, one cup at a time, mixing well after each addition.
    - Add the vanilla extract and beat until smooth and fluffy.
6. **Frost the cake (optional):**
    - Once the cake has cooled completely, spread the cream cheese frosting evenly over the top of the cake.
7. **Slice and serve:**
    - Slice the banana cake into squares and serve it as a delicious dessert or snack.

Tips:

- Make sure to use ripe bananas for the best flavor and sweetness in the cake.
- If you prefer, you can add chopped nuts (such as walnuts or pecans) or chocolate chips to the cake batter for extra texture and flavor.
- Store any leftover cake covered in the refrigerator. Bring it to room temperature before serving for the best texture and flavor.

This banana cake is moist, tender, and full of wonderful banana flavor. Whether you enjoy it plain or with cream cheese frosting, it's sure to be a favorite for banana lovers everywhere!

Pistachio and rosewater cake

Ingredients:

For the cake:

- 1 cup shelled pistachios (unsalted)
- 1 cup all-purpose flour
- 1 teaspoon baking powder
- 1/2 teaspoon baking soda
- 1/4 teaspoon salt
- 1/2 cup unsalted butter, softened
- 1 cup granulated sugar
- 3 large eggs
- 1/2 cup plain Greek yogurt (or sour cream)
- 2 tablespoons rosewater
- Zest of 1 lemon (optional, for added flavor)

For the rosewater syrup:

- 1/4 cup water
- 1/4 cup granulated sugar
- 2 tablespoons rosewater

For the rosewater glaze (optional):

- 1 cup powdered sugar (icing sugar)
- 1-2 tablespoons rosewater
- Chopped pistachios, for garnish

Instructions:

1. **Preheat your oven:**
   - Preheat the oven to 350°F (175°C). Grease and flour a 9-inch round cake pan, or line it with parchment paper for easy removal.
2. **Prepare the pistachios:**
   - In a food processor or blender, pulse the shelled pistachios until finely ground. Be careful not to over-process into a paste; you want a fine meal texture.
3. **Make the cake batter:**
   - In a medium bowl, whisk together the ground pistachios, flour, baking powder, baking soda, and salt. Set aside.
   - In a large mixing bowl, cream together the softened butter and granulated sugar until light and fluffy.
   - Add the eggs one at a time, beating well after each addition. Stir in the rosewater and lemon zest (if using).

- - Gradually add the dry ingredients to the creamed mixture, alternating with the Greek yogurt (or sour cream), beginning and ending with the dry ingredients. Mix until just combined.
4. **Bake the cake:**
   - Pour the batter into the prepared cake pan, spreading it out evenly with a spatula.
   - Bake in the preheated oven for 30-35 minutes, or until a toothpick inserted into the center comes out clean.
   - Remove from the oven and let the cake cool in the pan for 10 minutes before transferring it to a wire rack to cool completely.
5. **Make the rosewater syrup:**
   - In a small saucepan, combine the water and granulated sugar over medium heat. Stir until the sugar is dissolved.
   - Remove from heat and stir in the rosewater. Set aside to cool slightly.
6. **Poke holes and apply syrup:**
   - While the cake is still warm, use a toothpick or skewer to poke holes all over the top of the cake.
   - Slowly drizzle the rosewater syrup over the cake, allowing it to soak into the holes and absorb.
7. **Make the rosewater glaze (optional):**
   - In a small bowl, whisk together the powdered sugar and rosewater until smooth. Adjust the consistency by adding more rosewater if needed.
8. **Glaze the cake (optional):**
   - Once the cake has cooled completely and the syrup has been absorbed, drizzle the rosewater glaze over the top of the cake.
9. **Garnish and serve:**
   - Sprinkle chopped pistachios over the top of the cake for added texture and visual appeal.
   - Slice and serve the pistachio and rosewater cake. Enjoy the unique combination of nutty pistachios with delicate floral notes from the rosewater!

Tips:

- Ensure the pistachios are finely ground to achieve a smooth texture in the cake.
- Rosewater can vary in intensity, so adjust the amount to suit your preference for the floral flavor.
- This cake pairs wonderfully with a cup of tea or coffee and is perfect for special occasions or as a unique dessert option.

This pistachio and rosewater cake offers a delightful blend of flavors and textures that will impress your guests and satisfy your sweet tooth with its distinctive taste profile.

Carrot cake

Ingredients:

For the cake:

- 2 cups all-purpose flour
- 2 teaspoons baking powder
- 1 1/2 teaspoons baking soda
- 1/2 teaspoon salt
- 2 teaspoons ground cinnamon
- 1/2 teaspoon ground nutmeg
- 1/2 teaspoon ground ginger
- 1 cup granulated sugar
- 1 cup packed light brown sugar
- 1 cup vegetable oil (or canola oil)
- 4 large eggs
- 2 teaspoons vanilla extract
- 3 cups grated carrots (about 5-6 medium carrots)
- 1 cup crushed pineapple, drained (optional)
- 1 cup chopped nuts (walnuts or pecans), optional

For the cream cheese frosting:

- 8 oz (225g) cream cheese, softened
- 1/2 cup unsalted butter, softened
- 4 cups powdered sugar (icing sugar)
- 1 teaspoon vanilla extract

Optional garnish:

- Chopped nuts (walnuts or pecans)
- Shredded coconut
- Carrot decorations (made from marzipan or fondant)

Instructions:

1. **Preheat your oven:**
   - Preheat the oven to 350°F (175°C). Grease and flour two 9-inch round cake pans, or line them with parchment paper.
2. **Prepare the dry ingredients:**
   - In a medium bowl, whisk together the flour, baking powder, baking soda, salt, cinnamon, nutmeg, and ginger. Set aside.
3. **Mix the wet ingredients:**

- In a large mixing bowl, combine the granulated sugar, brown sugar, and vegetable oil. Mix well until combined.
- Add the eggs one at a time, mixing well after each addition. Stir in the vanilla extract.

4. **Combine dry and wet ingredients:**
   - Gradually add the dry ingredients to the wet ingredients, mixing until just combined. Do not overmix.
5. **Add carrots and optional ingredients:**
   - Fold in the grated carrots and crushed pineapple (if using). Add chopped nuts if desired.
6. **Bake the cake:**
   - Divide the batter evenly between the prepared cake pans, spreading it out evenly with a spatula.
   - Bake in the preheated oven for 25-30 minutes, or until a toothpick inserted into the center comes out clean.
   - Remove from the oven and let the cakes cool in the pans for 10 minutes before transferring them to a wire rack to cool completely.
7. **Make the cream cheese frosting:**
   - In a mixing bowl, beat together the softened cream cheese and butter until smooth and creamy.
   - Gradually add the powdered sugar, one cup at a time, mixing well after each addition.
   - Add the vanilla extract and beat until smooth and fluffy.
8. **Assemble the cake:**
   - Place one cooled cake layer on a serving plate or cake stand.
   - Spread a layer of cream cheese frosting evenly over the top of the cake layer.
   - Carefully place the second cake layer on top. Spread the remaining frosting evenly over the top and sides of the cake.
9. **Optional garnish:**
   - Garnish the cake with chopped nuts and shredded coconut, or decorate with carrot decorations made from marzipan or fondant.
10. **Chill and serve:**
    - Chill the cake in the refrigerator for about 30 minutes before slicing and serving. This helps set the frosting and makes it easier to slice.
11. **Slice and enjoy:**
    - Slice the carrot cake and serve it as a delightful dessert or treat. Enjoy the moist texture and spiced flavor of this classic favorite!

Tips:

- Make sure to grate the carrots finely for a smooth texture in the cake.
- If you prefer, you can omit the crushed pineapple or nuts, or adjust the amount according to your preference.

- Store any leftover cake covered in the refrigerator. Bring it to room temperature before serving for the best texture and flavor.

This carrot cake is perfect for celebrations, gatherings, or as a special treat any time of year. Its rich flavor and creamy frosting make it a crowd-pleaser that everyone will love!

Fig and almond cake

Ingredients:

For the cake:

- 1 cup all-purpose flour
- 1 teaspoon baking powder
- 1/4 teaspoon baking soda
- 1/4 teaspoon salt
- 1/2 cup unsalted butter, softened
- 1/2 cup granulated sugar
- 2 large eggs
- 1 teaspoon vanilla extract
- 1/2 cup almond meal (ground almonds)
- 1/2 cup plain Greek yogurt (or sour cream)
- 6-8 fresh figs, stems removed and sliced

For the topping:

- 6-8 fresh figs, stems removed and sliced
- 1/4 cup sliced almonds

Optional:

- Honey or maple syrup, for drizzling
- Powdered sugar (icing sugar), for dusting

Instructions:

1. **Preheat your oven:**
   - Preheat the oven to 350°F (175°C). Grease and flour a 9-inch round cake pan, or line it with parchment paper for easy removal.
2. **Prepare the dry ingredients:**
   - In a medium bowl, whisk together the flour, baking powder, baking soda, and salt. Set aside.
3. **Make the cake batter:**
   - In a large mixing bowl, cream together the softened butter and granulated sugar until light and fluffy.
   - Add the eggs one at a time, beating well after each addition. Stir in the vanilla extract.
   - Gradually add the almond meal (ground almonds) and mix until combined.
   - Add half of the dry ingredients to the batter, mixing until just combined. Then add the Greek yogurt (or sour cream), followed by the remaining dry ingredients, mixing until smooth.

4. **Assemble the cake:**
   - Pour the batter into the prepared cake pan, spreading it out evenly with a spatula.
   - Arrange the sliced figs evenly over the top of the batter.
5. **Add the topping:**
   - Scatter the sliced almonds over the figs on top of the cake batter.
6. **Bake the cake:**
   - Bake in the preheated oven for 30-35 minutes, or until a toothpick inserted into the center comes out clean.
   - Remove from the oven and let the cake cool in the pan for 10 minutes before transferring it to a wire rack to cool completely.
7. **Optional finishing touches:**
   - Once cooled, drizzle the top of the cake with honey or maple syrup for extra sweetness.
   - Dust with powdered sugar (icing sugar) for a decorative touch.
8. **Slice and serve:**
   - Slice the fig and almond cake and serve it as a delightful dessert or treat. Enjoy the combination of flavors and textures!

Tips:

- Use fresh figs for the best flavor and texture in the cake.
- You can adjust the sweetness by adding more or less sugar, depending on your preference and the sweetness of the figs.
- Serve the cake slightly warm or at room temperature for the best taste experience.

This fig and almond cake is perfect for showcasing fresh figs when they're in season. It's a wonderful dessert to enjoy with a cup of tea or coffee, or as a light and elegant ending to a meal.

Gingerbread

Ingredients:

- 2 1/2 cups all-purpose flour
- 2 teaspoons ground ginger
- 1 teaspoon ground cinnamon
- 1/4 teaspoon ground cloves
- 1/4 teaspoon ground nutmeg
- 1/2 teaspoon baking soda
- 1/2 teaspoon salt
- 1/2 cup unsalted butter, softened
- 1/2 cup brown sugar, packed
- 1 large egg
- 1/2 cup molasses
- 1/2 cup hot water

Optional icing (for decorating):

- 1 cup powdered sugar (icing sugar)
- 1-2 tablespoons milk or water
- 1/2 teaspoon vanilla extract

Instructions:

1. **Preheat your oven:**
   - Preheat the oven to 350°F (175°C). Grease and flour a 9-inch square baking pan, or line it with parchment paper.
2. **Prepare the dry ingredients:**
   - In a medium bowl, whisk together the flour, ground ginger, cinnamon, cloves, nutmeg, baking soda, and salt. Set aside.
3. **Make the gingerbread batter:**
   - In a large mixing bowl, cream together the softened butter and brown sugar until light and fluffy.
   - Beat in the egg until well combined.
   - Stir in the molasses until smooth.
4. **Combine wet and dry ingredients:**
   - Gradually add the dry ingredients to the creamed mixture, alternating with the hot water, beginning and ending with the dry ingredients. Mix until smooth and well combined.
5. **Bake the gingerbread:**
   - Pour the batter into the prepared baking pan, spreading it out evenly with a spatula.

- Bake in the preheated oven for 30-35 minutes, or until a toothpick inserted into the center comes out clean.
- Remove from the oven and let the gingerbread cool in the pan for 10 minutes before transferring it to a wire rack to cool completely.

6. **Optional icing (for decorating):**
   - In a small bowl, whisk together the powdered sugar, milk (or water), and vanilla extract until smooth and drizzle consistency.

7. **Decorate and serve:**
   - Once the gingerbread has cooled completely, drizzle or spread the icing over the top.
   - Slice the gingerbread into squares or rectangles and serve. Enjoy the warm spices and rich flavor of this traditional holiday treat!

Tips:

- For a stronger ginger flavor, you can increase the amount of ground ginger.
- If you prefer a softer texture, you can wrap the cooled gingerbread in plastic wrap overnight before serving.
- Gingerbread is delicious on its own, or served with a dollop of whipped cream or vanilla ice cream for a delightful dessert.

This gingerbread recipe is perfect for festive occasions or any time you're craving a comforting, spiced treat. Enjoy the aroma of ginger, cinnamon, and molasses as it fills your kitchen!

Rum ball cake

Ingredients:

For the cake:

- 1 cup unsalted butter, softened
- 1 cup granulated sugar
- 4 large eggs
- 1 teaspoon vanilla extract
- 2 cups all-purpose flour
- 1/2 cup cocoa powder
- 1 teaspoon baking powder
- 1/2 teaspoon baking soda
- 1/2 teaspoon salt
- 1 cup sour cream
- 1/4 cup dark rum

For the rum ball filling:

- 1 1/2 cups finely crushed chocolate wafer cookies (about 20 cookies)
- 1 cup finely chopped pecans or walnuts
- 1 cup powdered sugar (icing sugar)
- 1/4 cup dark rum
- 2 tablespoons light corn syrup
- 1/4 cup cocoa powder (for rolling the rum balls)

For the chocolate glaze:

- 1 cup semisweet chocolate chips
- 1/2 cup heavy cream

Instructions:

1. **Preheat your oven:**
    - Preheat the oven to 350°F (175°C). Grease and flour a 10-inch bundt pan, or use a non-stick baking spray.
2. **Prepare the cake batter:**
    - In a large mixing bowl, cream together the softened butter and granulated sugar until light and fluffy.
    - Add the eggs one at a time, beating well after each addition. Stir in the vanilla extract.
    - In a separate bowl, sift together the flour, cocoa powder, baking powder, baking soda, and salt.

- Gradually add the dry ingredients to the creamed mixture, alternating with the sour cream and rum. Begin and end with the dry ingredients, mixing until just combined.

3. **Bake the cake:**
    - Pour the batter into the prepared bundt pan, spreading it out evenly with a spatula.
    - Bake in the preheated oven for 50-60 minutes, or until a toothpick inserted into the center comes out clean.
    - Remove from the oven and let the cake cool in the pan for 10 minutes before transferring it to a wire rack to cool completely.

4. **Make the rum ball filling:**
    - In a large mixing bowl, combine the finely crushed chocolate wafer cookies, chopped nuts, and powdered sugar.
    - Stir in the dark rum and light corn syrup until the mixture comes together. It should be firm enough to form into balls.
    - Shape the mixture into small balls, about 1 inch in diameter. Roll each ball in cocoa powder to coat evenly. Place the rum balls on a baking sheet lined with parchment paper and refrigerate for about 30 minutes to firm up.

5. **Make the chocolate glaze:**
    - In a small saucepan, heat the heavy cream until it just begins to simmer.
    - Remove from heat and pour over the semisweet chocolate chips in a heatproof bowl. Let it sit for 2-3 minutes, then stir until smooth and glossy.

6. **Assemble the cake:**
    - Once the cake has cooled completely, place it on a serving plate or cake stand.
    - Arrange the rum balls on top of the cake, pressing them lightly into the surface.
    - Drizzle the chocolate glaze over the cake and rum balls, allowing it to drip down the sides.

7. **Chill and serve:**
    - Chill the cake in the refrigerator for about 30 minutes to set the chocolate glaze.

8. **Slice and enjoy:**
    - Slice the rum ball cake and serve it as a decadent and festive dessert. The combination of chocolate, rum, and crunchy rum balls makes it a delightful treat for special occasions!

Tips:

- Ensure the cake is completely cooled before adding the rum balls and chocolate glaze to prevent melting.
- Store any leftover cake in an airtight container in the refrigerator. Bring it to room temperature before serving for the best texture and flavor.
- You can adjust the amount of rum in the rum ball filling according to your preference for a stronger or milder rum flavor.

This rum ball cake is sure to impress with its rich flavors and beautiful presentation. It's perfect for holiday gatherings, celebrations, or anytime you want to indulge in a decadent dessert!

www.ingramcontent.com/pod-product-compliance
Lightning Source LLC
LaVergne TN
LVHW081555060526
838201LV00054B/1905